TEACHER'S PET PUBLICATIONS

LITPLAN TEACHER PACK
for
Siddhartha
based on the novel by
Hermann Hesse

Written by
Susan Woodward

© 2008 Teacher's Pet Publications
All Rights Reserved

Copyright Teacher's Pet Publications 2008

Only the student materials in this unit plan (such as worksheets, study questions, and tests) may be reproduced multiple times for use in the purchaser's classroom.

For any additional copyright questions, contact Teacher's Pet Publications.

www.tpet.com

TABLE OF CONTENTS
Siddhartha

Introduction	5
Unit Objectives	7
Reading Assignment Sheet	8
Unit Outline	9
Study Questions (Short Answer)	13
Quiz/Study Questions (Multiple Choice)	20
Pre-reading Vocabulary Worksheets	35
Lesson One (Introductory Lesson)	51
Oral Reading Evaluation Form	71
Writing Assignment #1	57
Writing Evaluation Form	111
Non-fiction Assignment Sheet	69
Writing Assignment #2	98
Writing Assignment #3	107
Extra Writing Assignments/Discussion ?s	102
Vocabulary Review Activities	88
Unit Review Activities	112
Unit Tests	119
Unit Resource Materials	165
Vocabulary Resource Materials	183

ABOUT THE AUTHOR

Hermann Hesse

Hermann Hesse, a German writer, was born in Calw in the Black Forest on July 2, 1877. He was the son of Jahannes Hesse and Marie Gundert, both from missionary families. It was their hope that their son would follow in the family tradition of theology, and in his own way, he did. His novels explored the duality of spirit and nature as well as the individual's spiritual search outside the restrictions of society. Studying and undergoing psychoanalysis under J.B. Lang, assistant to the Swiss psychologist Carl Jung, led Hesse to depict the protagonist's journey into the inner self in many of his novels. In several of his works, a spiritual guide assists the hero in his quest for self-knowledge. For this work, Hesse was awarded the Nobel Prize for Literature in 1946.

While working as a bookshop clerk and a book dealer in Tubingen, Hesse joined a literary circle called Le Petit Cenacle. Through his association with this circle, Hesse became determined to become a writer. His first published works were *Romantische Lieder* and *Eine Stunde Hinter Mitternacht* 1899. His first true success came in 1904 when his novel *Peter Camenzind* about a young man who leaves his life in the big city in order to live like St. Francis of Assisi.

After a trip to India in 1911, Hesse became interested in studying Eastern religion, which led to *Siddhartha* (1922), a fictional account of the life of Buddha, Siddhartha Gautama. The culture of ancient Hindu and the ancient Chinese had a great influence on Hesse's works.

Hermann Hesse married three times throughout his life. His first wife was photographer Maria Bernoulli (married 1904), with whom he had his three sons. After his wife suffered from severe mental disabilities and his youngest son became extremely ill, he and Maria eventually divorced in 1924. He was then briefly married to Ruth Wenger, the daughter of Swiss writer Lisa Wenger, in 1924. The marriage only lasted several months. In 1931, Hesse married Ninon Dolbin with whom he stayed until his death in 1962.

The influence of Carl Jung was expressed in Hesse's *Demian* (1919) for which he earned critical acclaim. Much like 1922's *Siddhartha*, *Demian*'s protagonist is torn between his orderly bourgeois existence and a chaotic world of sensuality. This Jungian process of individuation faced by his characters mirrors Hesse's own journey through life.

Other important works include *Der Steppenwolf* (1927), form which the California rock band took its name, and what has been touted as his masterpiece, 1943's *Das Glasperlenspiel* (The Glass Bead Game). The band Steppenwolf released the song "Born to be Wild" in 1968 reflecting how *Der Steppenwolf*'s protagonist, Harry Haller, goes through his mid-life crisis and must choose between life of action and contemplation. The setting of *Das Glasperlenspiel* is in the future in the imaginary province of Castilia, an intellectual, elitist community, dedicated to mathematics and music. The novel is the story of Knecht's search for wisdom and his eventual rise to Magister Lundi, "The Master of the Games."

Hermann Hesse died peacefully in his sleep on August 9, 1962 from a cerebral hemorrhage at the age of eighty-five.

INTRODUCTION *Siddhartha*

This LitPlan has been designed to develop students' reading, writing, thinking, and language skills through exercises and activities related to *Siddhartha* by Hermann Hesse. It includes seventeen lessons, supported by extra resource materials.

The **introductory lesson** introduces students to Joseph Campbell's Hero's Journey. Following the introductory activity, students are given a transition to explain how the activity relates to the book they are about to read. Following the transition, students are given the materials they will be using during the unit. At the end of the lesson, students begin the pre-reading work for the first reading assignment.

The **reading assignments** are approximately thirty pages each; some are a little shorter while others are a little longer. Students have approximately 15 minutes of pre-reading work to do prior to each reading assignment. This pre-reading work involves reviewing the study questions for the assignment and doing some vocabulary work for selected vocabulary words they will encounter in their reading.

The **study guide questions** are fact-based questions; students can find the answers to these questions right in the text. These questions come in two formats: short answer or multiple choice. The best use of these materials is probably to use the short answer version of the questions as study guides for students (since answers will be more complete), and to use the multiple choice version for occasional quizzes.

The **vocabulary work** is intended to enrich students' vocabularies as well as to aid in the students' understanding of the book. Prior to each reading assignment, students will complete a two-part worksheet for selected vocabulary words in the upcoming reading assignment. Part I focuses on students' use of general knowledge and contextual clues by giving the sentence in which the word appears in the text. Students are then to write down what they think the words mean based on the words' usage. Part II nails down the definitions of the words by giving students dictionary definitions of the words and having students match the words to the correct definitions based on the words' contextual usage. Students should then have an understanding of the words when they meet them in the text.

After each reading assignment, students will go back and formulate answers for the study guide questions. Discussion of these questions serves as a **review** of the most important events and ideas presented in the reading assignments.

After students complete reading the work, there is a **vocabulary review** lesson which pulls together all of the fragmented vocabulary lists for the reading assignments and gives students a review of all of the words they have studied.

Following the vocabulary review, a lesson is devoted to the **extra discussion questions/writing assignments**. These questions focus on interpretation, critical analysis, and personal response, employing a variety of thinking skills and adding to the students' understanding of the novel.

There are three **writing assignments** in this unit, each with the purpose of informing, persuading, or expressing personal opinions. Introspection journal entries will be converted into a poetic reflection of the students' personal journeys towards self-knowledge. Students will also complete a poetry analysis and relate the poets' messages to themes in *Siddhartha*. In the persuasive assignment, students will take a position on Siddhartha's decision regarding his son and defend the position with textual support from the novel and the Four Noble Truths.

There is a non-fiction **reading assignment**. Students must read non-fiction articles, books, etc. to gather information about their themes in our world today.

The **review lesson** pulls together all of the aspects of the unit. The teacher is given four or five choices of activities or games to use which all serve the same basic function of reviewing all of the information presented in the unit.

The **unit test** comes in two formats: multiple choice or short answer. As a convenience, two different tests for each format have been included. There is also an advanced short answer unit test for advanced students.

There are additional **support materials** included with this unit. The **Unit Resource Materials** section includes suggestions for an in-class library, crossword and word search puzzles related to the novel, and extra worksheets. There is a list of **bulletin board ideas** which gives the teacher suggestions for bulletin boards to go along with this unit. In addition, there is a list of **extra class activities** the teacher could choose from to enhance the unit or as a substitution for an exercise the teacher might feel is inappropriate for his/her class. **Answer keys** are located directly after the **reproducible student materials** throughout the unit. The **Vocabulary Resource Materials** section includes similar worksheets and games to reinforce the vocabulary words.

The **level** of this unit can be varied depending upon the criteria on which the individual assignments are graded, the teacher's expectations of his/her students in class discussions, and the formats chosen for the study guides, quizzes and test. If teachers have other ideas/activities they wish to use, they can usually easily be inserted prior to the review lesson.

The student materials may be reproduced for use in the teacher's classroom without infringement of copyrights. No other portion of this unit may be reproduced without the written consent of Teacher's Pet Publications, Inc.

UNIT OBJECTIVES *Siddhartha*

1. While reading Hermann Hesse's *Siddhartha*, students will work both independently and in cooperative groups.

2. Students will demonstrate their understanding of the text on four levels: factual, interpretive, critical, and personal.

3. Students will spend time in personal reflection, examining their own personal growth and self-knowledge.

4. Students will practice reading aloud and silently to improve their skills in each area.

5. Students will answer questions to demonstrate their knowledge and understanding of the main events and characters in *Siddhartha* as they relate to the author's theme development.

6. Students will enrich their vocabularies and improve their understanding of the novel through the vocabulary lessons prepared for use in conjunction with the novel.

7. The writing assignments are geared to several purposes:
    a. To have students demonstrate their abilities to inform, persuade, express their own personal ideas, or be creative
    b. To check students' reading comprehension
    c. To make students think about ideas presented in the novel
    d. To encourage logical thinking
    e. To provide an opportunity for students to practice good grammar and improve their use of standard, written English

8. Students will read aloud, report, and participate in large and small group discussions to improve their public speaking and personal interaction skills.

READING ASSIGNMENTS *Siddhartha*

Date Assigned	Assignment	Completion Date
	Assignment 1 Chapters 1-2	
	Assignment 2 Chapters 3-4	
	Assignment 3 Chapters 5-6	
	Assignment 4 Chapters 7-8	
	Assignment 5 Chapters 9-10	
	Assignment 6 Chapters 11-12	

UNIT OUTLINE *Siddhartha*

1	2	3	4	5
Introduce Hero's Journey Begin Journal Entries (WA#1) PVR Ch 1-2	Study ?s 1-2 Characterization & Departure Stage PVR Ch 3-4	Study ?s 3-4 Quiz Ch 1-4 Nonfiction Work PVR Ch 5-6	Study ?s 5-6 PV Ch 7-8 Read Aloud Ch 7-8	Study ?s Ch 7-8 Quiz Ch 5-8 4 Noble Truths & 8-Fold Noble Path PVR 9-10
6 Study ?s 9-10 Initiation Stage PVR Ch 11-12	**7** Study ?s 11-12 Quiz Ch 9-12 Return Stage	**8** Vocabulary Work	**9** Poetry Analysis Writing Assignment #2	**10** Figurative Language Exercises
11 Creative Writing Day 1: Planning with a Partner	**12** Creative Writing Day 2: Composing the Poem	**13** Group Work: Extra Discussion Questions	**14** In-Class Writing: Writing Assignment #3	**15** Peer Editing and Revision: WA #3
16 Review Materials	**17** Unit Test	**18** Open Mike: Share Poems (Optional)		

Key: P = Preview Study Questions   V = Vocabulary Work   R = Read

STUDY GUIDE QUESTIONS

STUDY GUIDE QUESTIONS *Siddhartha*

Assignment 1
Chapters 1-2
1. Who is Govinda?
2. How do the people of Siddhartha's home town feel about him?
3. What has caused Siddhartha "to feel the seeds of discontent within him"?
4. When Siddhartha first leaves home, where does he want to go to try to acquire more knowledge?
5. Who accompanies Siddhartha on his journey to become Samana?
6. What changes that take place in Siddhartha while on the road with the Samanas?
7. What is Siddhartha's "one single goal" on his first journey?
8. With what two animals did Siddhartha associate himself through practicing "self-denial and meditation according to the Samana rules"?
9. Identify Gotama.
10. How does Siddhartha prove that he has mastered all that the Samana could teach him?

Assignment 2
Chapters 3-4
1. What is Jetavana?
2. By what qualities do Siddhartha and Govinda recognize the Buddha?
3. Why is Siddhartha not very curious about the teachings of the Buddha?
4. What is Siddhartha's response to Govinda's question about following the Buddha?
5. What does the Buddha warn Siddhartha to be on his guard against?
6. What separates Govinda and Siddhartha?
7. What does Siddhartha realize has left him "like the old skin that a snake sheds"?
8. What realization gives Siddhartha the feeling of awakening from a long dream?
9. After Siddhartha decides not to join the Buddha's community, from whom does he choose to learn?
10. After Siddhartha leaves Jetavana grove, where does he initially intend to go?

Assignment 3
Chapters 5-6
1. When Siddhartha decides to be "present" in the world, what does he begin to notice about it?
2. After leaving the presence of the Buddha, what is it that Siddhartha believes he must gain for himself?
3. What does Siddhartha's dream as he slept in the ferryman's straw hut.
4. The ferryman tells Siddhartha that one can learn much from something. What?
5. When Siddhartha is tempted by the woman in the village, what stops him from proceeding?
6. Who is Kamala?

7. Who is Kamaswami? Why does Kamala send Siddhartha to him?
8. What services does Siddhartha say he can perform for Kamaswami?
9. What is Siddhartha's attitude toward business?
10. To what does Siddhartha compare those who have no "stillness and sanctuary to which [they] can retreat at any time"?

Assignment 4
Chapters 7-8

1. What becomes of Siddhartha's "glorious, exalted awakening" that he had experienced in his youth?
2. When Siddhartha's soul goes to sleep, what becomes more awakened?
3. What are some of the things Siddhartha learns to do while living in the town after meeting Kamala and Kamaswami?
4. In what game does Siddhartha become increasingly involved?
5. What does Siddhartha dream when he becomes dissatisfied with his gambling life?
6. What discovery does Kamala make after the disappearance of Siddhartha?
7. For what does Siddhartha passionately wish when he leaves Kamala and the town?
8. What sound comes to Siddhartha that awakens his "slumbering soul"?
9. Who does Siddhartha see when he awakes from his long sleep?
10. What things does Siddhartha claim he has had to experience "just in order to become a child again and begin anew"?

Assignment 5
Chapters 9-10

1. What is it that brings Siddhartha feelings of love, enchantment, and gratitude?
2. Who is Vasudeva?
3. What is the first "secret from the river" that Siddhartha learns?
4. What one word does the river pronounce "when one is successful in hearing all its ten thousand voices at the same time"?
5. What becomes of Kamala?
6. How does Siddhartha's son behave while living in the hut by the river?
7. What does Vasudeva suggest Siddhartha should do for his son?
8. What is the boy's reaction when Siddhartha asks him to gather some twigs for the fire?
9. Siddhartha tries to find his son after he runs away. Why does Siddhartha stop his search at the garden that has once belonged to Kamala?

Assignment 6
Chapters 11-12

1. What knowledge does Siddhartha possess that he many times "doubted...was of such great value?"
2. When Siddhartha bends over the water of the river and sees his reflection, of whose face is he reminded?
3. To what realization does Siddhartha come after seeing his reflection in the water?
4. After listening to the song of the river, where does Vasudeva go?
5. Who hears tales about the old ferryman by the river and decides to go see him?
6. According to Siddhartha, what is the difference between seeking and finding?
7. What does Siddhartha hold in his hand and tell Govinda that it may one day possibly become either a plant, an animal, or a man?
8. What does Govinda claim that the Illustrious One called illusion and forbade his followers to bind themselves?
9. What does Govinda see in Siddhartha's face?

STUDY GUIDE QUESTIONS ANSWER KEY *Siddhartha*

Assignment 1
Chapters 1-2

1. Who is Govinda?
   Govinda is Siddhartha's friend. He is the son of a Brahmin.
2. How do the people of Siddhartha's home town feel about him?
   The townspeople admire and love Siddhartha.
3. What has caused Siddhartha "to feel the seeds of discontent within him"?
   Siddhartha believes that he has obtained all the knowledge that his father and teachers can offer, but it is not enough.
4. When Siddhartha first leaves home, where does he want to go to try to acquire more knowledge?
   He wants to travel with the ascetics and become a Samana.
5. Who accompanies Siddhartha on his journey to become Samana?
   Govinda accompanies Siddhartha.
6. What changes take place in Siddhartha while on the road with the Samanas?
   He becomes thin from fasting, his nails grow long, he gives away his clothes, he snarls at women, and he looks at well-dressed people with contempt.
7. What is Siddhartha's "one single goal" on his first journey?
   He wishes to let the Self die.
8. With what two animals did Siddhartha associate himself through practicing "self-denial and meditation according to the Samana rules"?
   Siddhartha compares himself to the heron and the jackal.
9. Identify Gotama.
   Gotama is the Illustrious One, the Buddha who has reportedly attained Nirvana and wanders the countryside preaching. Govinda follows him, but Siddhartha chooses not to.
10. How does Siddhartha prove that he has mastered all that the Samana could teach him?
    Siddhartha hypnotizes the eldest Samana, proving that he has mastered all that the Samana could teach him.

Assignment 2
Chapters 3-4

1. What is Jetavana?
   It is the Buddha's favorite place to stay, which had been given to him by Anathapindika.
2. By what qualities do Siddhartha and Govinda recognize the Buddha?
   They recognize him only by his complete peacefulness of demeanor, by the stillness of his form, in which there was no seeking, no will, no counterfeit, no effort--only light and peace.
3. Why is Siddhartha not very curious about the teachings of the Buddha?
   He does not think the Buddha can teach him anything new.
4. What is Siddhartha's response to Govinda's question about following the Buddha?
   Siddhartha blesses Govinda and wishes him well but says he will not be joining the Buddha's company.
5. What does the Buddha warn Siddhartha to be on his guard against?
   The Buddha warns Siddhartha to be on his guard against too much cleverness.

6. What separates Govinda and Siddhartha?
   Govinda joins the Buddha's community, and Siddhartha moves on.
7. What does Siddhartha realize has left him "like the old skin that a snake sheds"?
   He has lost the desire to have teachers and to listen to their teaching.
8. What realization gives Siddhartha the feeling of awakening from a long dream?
   He realizes he has been afraid of being himself, and so he has tried to lose himself in the teachings of others.
9. After Siddhartha decides not to join the Buddha's community, from whom does he choose to learn?
   He chooses to learn from himself.
10. After Siddhartha leaves Jetavana grove, where does he initially intend to go?
    He initially intends to go home to see his father.

Assignment 3
Chapters 5-6
1. When Siddhartha decides to be "present" in the world, what does he begin to notice about it?
   He notices the beauty of nature that he had never paid attention to before.
2. After leaving the presence of the Buddha, what is it that Siddhartha believes he must gain for himself?
   He believes he must gain experience.
3. What does Siddhartha dream as he slept in the ferryman's straw hut?
   Siddhartha dreams that Govinda stands before him asking, "Why did you leave me?" Govinda then turns into a woman from whose breast Siddhartha drinks and becomes intoxicated with pleasure.
4. The ferryman tells Siddhartha that one can learn much from something. What?
   The ferryman tells Siddhartha that one can learn much from a river.
5. When Siddhartha is tempted by the woman in the village, what stops him from proceeding?
   Siddhartha hears his inward voice say, "No!"
6. Who is Kamala?
   Kamala is a beautiful courtesan from whom Siddhartha wishes to learn about the art of love.
7. Who is Kamaswami? Why does Kamala send Siddhartha to him?
   Kamaswami is the richest merchant in town. Kamala insists that Siddhartha must see him so that he may gain fine clothes, shoes, and money. Only then will Siddhartha be fit to be with Kamala.
8. What services does Siddhartha say he can perform for Kamaswami?
   Siddhartha tells Kamaswami that he can think, he can wait, and he can fast.
9. What is Siddhartha's attitude toward business?
   Siddhartha is indifferent towards business and unconcerned about making a profit.
10. To what does Siddhartha compare those who have no "stillness and sanctuary to which [they] can retreat at any time"?
    Siddhartha compares them to falling leaves that drift and turn in the air but have no direction.

Assignment 4
Chapters 7-8

1. What becomes of Siddhartha's "glorious, exalted awakening" that he had experienced in his youth?
   It becomes a memory and passes away.

2. When Siddhartha's soul goes to sleep, what becomes more awakened?
   His senses become heightened.

3. What are some of the things Siddhartha learns to do while living in the town after meeting Kamala and Kamaswami?
   He learns to transact business, exercise power over people, amuse himself with women, wear fine clothes, command servants, bathe in sweet-smelling waters, eat rich foods, and drink wine.

4. In what game does Siddhartha become increasingly involved?
   He becomes increasingly involved with dice, gambling for money and jewels.

5. What does Siddhartha dream when he becomes dissatisfied with his gambling life?
   He dreams that Kamala's bird dies in its cage, and he throws it away on the road. He is horrified by this and feels as if he has thrown away what is good and of value in himself.

6. What discovery does Kamala make after the disappearance of Siddhartha?
   She discovers she is pregnant with his child.

7. For what does Siddhartha passionately wish when he leaves Kamala and the town?
   He wishes for death and tries to commit suicide.

8. What sound comes to Siddhartha that awakens his "slumbering soul"?
   He hears, "Om."

9. Who does Siddhartha see when he awakes from his long sleep?
   He sees a monk in a yellow gown and realizes it is Govinda.

10. What things does Siddhartha claim he has had to experience "just in order to become a child again and begin anew"?
    He has had to experience stupidity, vices, error, nausea, disillusionment, and sorrow.

Assignment 5
Chapters 9-10

1. What is it that brings Siddhartha feelings of love, enchantment, and gratitude?
   His love for the flowing river brings him these feelings.

2. Who is Vasudeva?
   Vasudeva is the ferryman who takes Siddhartha into his service.

3. What is the first "secret from the river" that Siddhartha learns?
   He learns that there is no such thing as time. "The river is everywhere at the same time, at the source and at the mouth, at the waterfall, at the ferry, at the current, in the ocean, and in the mountains, everywhere, and that the present only exists for it."

4. What one word does the river pronounce "when one is successful in hearing all its ten thousand voices at the same time"?
   The river says, "Om."

5. What becomes of Kamala?
   She is bitten by a snake while on a pilgrimage to see the dying Buddha; she dies.

6. How does Siddhartha's son behave while living in the hut by the river?
   He is a spoiled rich boy who refuses to do any work, and he is disrespectful of others.

7. What does Vasudeva suggest Siddhartha should do for his son?
   Vasudeva suggests that Siddhartha should take the boy back to the town where he grew up and find him a life that includes people his own age.
8. What is the boy's reaction when Siddhartha asks him to gather some twigs for the fire?
   He refuses and then goes on to tell Siddhartha how much he hates his father. The boy runs away the next day.
9. Siddhartha tries to find his son after he runs away. Why does Siddhartha stop his search at the garden that had once belonged to Kamala?
   Standing at the garden Siddhartha remembered his life and in doing so he realized it was a foolish desire to follow his son. He realizes that he can not help his son and that he shouldn't force himself on his son.

Assignment 6
Chapters 11-12
1. What knowledge does Siddhartha possess that he many times "doubted...was of such great value?"
   He possesses the consciousness of the unity of life, but he has begun to think that it is "perhaps the childish self-flattery of thinkers, who were perhaps only thinking children."
2. When Siddhartha bends over the water of the river and sees his reflection, of whose face is he reminded?
   He is reminded of his father's face when he sees his own reflection.
3. To what realization does Siddhartha come after seeing his reflection in the water?
   He realizes that his father had suffered the same sorrows at Siddhartha's leaving that Siddhartha now suffers at the leaving of his own son.
4. After listening to the song of the river, where does Vasudeva go?
   He goes into the woods to die.
5. Who hears tales about the old ferryman by the river and decides to go see him?
   Govinda hears the tales and decides to go see the old ferryman.
6. According to Siddhartha, what is the difference between seeking and finding?
   To seek means to have a goal; to find means to be receptive without a goal.
7. What does Siddhartha hold in his hand and tell Govinda that it may one day possibly become either a plant, an animal, or a man?
   He holds a stone, which within a certain amount of time may break down to become soil, and then may become a plant, an animal, or a man.
8. What does Govinda claim that the Illustrious One called illusion and forbade his followers to bind themselves?
   He forbade them to bind themselves to love.
9. What does Govinda see in Siddhartha's face?
   When Govinda looks into Siddhartha's face, he sees many other faces--hundreds, thousands, which seemed to be there all at the same time, and yet were all Siddhartha.

MULTIPLE CHOICE STUDY/QUIZ QUESTIONS
Siddhartha

Assignment 1
Chapters 1-2

1. Who is Govinda?
    A. Govinda is Siddhartha's teacher.
    B. Govinda is Siddhartha's father.
    C. Govinda is the town's Brahmin.
    D. Govinda is Siddhartha's childhood friend.

2. How do the people of Siddhartha's home town feel about him?
    A. They think he is a spoiled child.
    B. The townspeople admire and love Siddhartha.
    C. They want to make him the new Brahmin.
    D. They are jealous of the Brahmin's attentions towards him.

3. What has caused Siddhartha "to feel the seeds of discontent within him"?
    A. Siddhartha desires to travel to see far away lands.
    B. Siddhartha wishes to attend a university.
    C. Siddhartha believes that he has obtained all the knowledge that his father and teachers can offer, but it is not enough.
    D. Siddhartha cannot find his one true love.

4. When Siddhartha first leaves home, where does he want to go to try to acquire more knowledge?
    A. He wants to follow the Buddha and learn all the Buddha has to teach.
    B. He wants to travel with the ascetics and become a Samana.
    C. He wants to go to China.
    D. He wants to go to the University of Padua.

5. Who accompanies Siddhartha on his journey to become a Samana?
    A. Siddhartha's younger brother accompanies with him.
    B. Siddhartha's father accompanies with him.
    C. Govinda accompanies Siddhartha.
    D. Siddhartha's future bride accompanies with him.

6. Which is NOT a change that takes place in Siddhartha while on the road with the Samanas?
    A. He looks at well-dressed people with contempt.
    B. His nails grow long.
    C. He snarls at women.
    D. He becomes fat from over-indulging in food.

7. What is Siddhartha's "one single goal" on his first journey?
    A. He wishes to let the Self die.
    B. He wishes to see the whole world.
    C. He wishes to find enlightenment.
    D. He wishes to find his one true love.

8. With what two animals did Siddhartha associate himself through practicing "self-denial and meditation according to the Samana rules"?
    A. The dove and the eagle
    B. The heron and the jackal
    C. The deer and the bear
    D. The eagle and the heron

9. Identify Gotama.
    A. Gotama is Siddhartha's father, the Holy One.
    B. Gotama is the head of Siddhartha's group of Samanas.
    C. Gotama is the Illustrious One, the Buddha who has reportedly achieved Nirvana.
    D. Gotama is Siddhartha's friend who follows the Buddha.

10. How does Siddhartha prove that he has mastered all that the Samana can teach him?
    A. Siddhartha reads the old man's mind.
    B. Siddhartha hypnotizes the eldest Samana.
    C. Siddhartha fasts for seven days.
    D. Siddhartha prays and makes it rain.

Assignment 2
Chapters 3-4

1. What is Jetavana?
    A. It is a prayer recited by the Samanas each evening.
    B. It is a trance-like state of euphoria.
    C. It is the name of the town where Siddhartha grew up.
    D. It is the Buddha's favorite place to stay.

2. By what qualities do Siddhartha and Govinda recognize the Buddha?
    A. They recognize him by the wisdom in his eyes and his aura of tranquility.
    B. They recognize him by his choice of clothing and his euphoric expression.
    C. They recognize him only by his complete sense of peacefulness and calm.
    D. They recognize him by his robe and staff.

3. Why is Siddhartha not very curious about the teachings of the Buddha?
    A. Since the Buddha is not a Samana, Siddhartha does not care to listen to him.
    B. Siddhartha has not heard of the Buddha.
    C. He does not agree with what the Buddha teaches.
    D. He does not think the Buddha can teach him anything new.

4. What is Siddhartha's response to Govinda's question about following the Buddha?
    A. Siddhartha blesses Govinda, wishes him well, and says he will not go with Govinda to follow the Buddha.
    B. He agrees with Govinda, and they both prepare to leave the Samanas to follow the Buddha.
    C. He becomes angry with Govinda for wanting to leave the Samanas.
    D. He says, "What is a Buddha?"

5. What does the Buddha warn Siddhartha to be on his guard against?
    A. False teachers
    B. Greed
    C. Loose women
    D. Too much cleverness

6. What separates Govinda and Siddhartha?
    A. Govinda is discouraged and leaves the Samanas for a life of the senses.
    B. Siddhartha returns to his home village.
    C. Siddhartha is bitten by a poisonous snake and dies.
    D. Govinda joins the Buddha's community.

7. What does Siddhartha realize has left him "like the old skin that a snake sheds"?
    A. He has lost the desire to have teachers and to listen to their teaching.
    B. His soul has left him unfulfilled.
    C. He has lost his friendship with Govinda.
    D. He has lost his sense of Self while traveling with the Samanas.

8. What realization gives Siddhartha the feeling of awakening from a long dream?
    A. After meeting women, he realizes what he has missed by denying his senses.
    B. He realizes he has been afraid of being himself, and so he has tried to lose himself in the teachings of others.
    C. He realizes how foolish the Buddha's teaching are.
    D. He realizes that he needs to return home to ask for his father's forgiveness.

9. After Siddhartha decides not to join the Buddha's community, from whom does he choose to learn?
    A. He chooses to learn from the university.
    B. He chooses to learn from his father.
    C. He chooses to learn from Govinda.
    D. He chooses to learn from himself.

10. After Siddhartha leaves Jetavana grove, where does he initially intend to go?
    A. He intends to follow the Buddha.
    B. He intends to go seek peace in the mountains.
    C. He intends to find a wife.
    D. He intends to go home to see his father.

Assignment 3
Chapters 5-6

1. When Siddhartha decides to be "present" in the world, what does he begin to notice about it?
   A. He notices the beauty of nature that he had never paid attention to before.
   B. He notices how large the world really is outside of his little village.
   C. He notices the ugliness of what man has done to nature.
   D. He notices how petty people act towards each other.

2. After leaving the presence of the Buddha, what is it that Siddhartha believes he must gain for himself?
   A. Enlightenment
   B. Love
   C. Money
   D. Experience

3. What does Siddhartha dream as he slept in the ferryman's straw hut?
   A. He dreams he floats along the river on a raft made of gold.
   B. He dreams Govinda becomes a woman and he drinks from her breast.
   C. He dreams his father dies.
   D. He dreams he drowns in the river.

4. The ferryman tells Siddhartha that one can learn from something. What?
   A. Money
   B. A river
   C. Love
   D. Dreams

5. When Siddhartha is tempted by the woman in the village, what stops him from proceeding?
   A. Siddhartha hears his inward voice say, "No!"
   B. Govinda came in.
   C. The woman's husband came home.
   D. He realizes he does not love the woman.

6. Who is Kamala?
   A. Kamala is a rich merchant who teaches Siddhartha about business.
   B. Kamala is a ferryman who tells Siddhartha secrets of the river.
   C. Kamala is the real name of the Buddha.
   D. Kamala is a beautiful courtesan who teaches Siddhartha about love.

7. Who is Kamaswami?
   A. Kamaswami is the real name of the Buddha.
   B. Kamaswami is a courtesan.
   C. Kamaswami is a ferryman.
   D. Kamaswami is a rich merchant.

8. What services does Siddhartha say he can perform for Kamaswami?
   A. He can do accounting and bookkeeping.
   B. He can learn to love.
   C. He can guide the ferry across the river.
   D. He can think, he can wait, and he can fast.

9. What is Siddhartha's attitude toward business?
   A. Siddhartha thinks business is bad for the soul.
   B. Siddhartha is indifferent towards business and unconcerned about making a profit.
   C. Siddhartha is more concerned about doing the right thing and helping others than making a profit.
   D. Siddhartha meticulous in his business dealings and accounting.

10. To what does Siddhartha compare those who have no "stillness and sanctuary to which [they] can retreat at any time"?
    A. He compares them to a heron flying high in the sky.
    B. He compares them to a snake shedding its skin.
    C. He compares them to falling leaves that have no direction.
    D. He compares them to the flowing river.

Assignment 4
Chapters 7-8

1. What becomes of Siddhartha's "glorious, exalted awakening" that he had experienced in his youth?

    A. It becomes a memory and passes away.

    B. It gnaws at his consciousness.

    C. It blossoms into fruition.

    D. It stays alive in his dreams.

2. When Siddhartha's soul goes to sleep, what becomes more awakened?

    A. His senses

    B. His enlightenment

    C. His consciousness

    D. His intellect

3. Which is NOT one of the things Siddhartha learns to do while living in the town after meeting Kamala and Kamaswami?

    A. He learns to exercise power over people.

    B. He learns to command servants.

    C. He learns to build elaborate temples.

    D. He learns to drink wine.

4. In what game does Siddhartha become increasingly involved?

    A. Cards

    B. Chess

    C. Jousting

    D. Dice

5. What does Siddhartha dream when he becomes dissatisfied with his gambling life?

    A. He dreams that Govinda becomes a woman, and he is attracted to him.

    B. He dreams that he becomes the Buddha and lives a life of peace.

    C. He dreams that Kamala's bird dies in its cage, and he throws it away on the road.

    D. He dreams that his father is displeased with him and dies of a broken heart.

6. What discovery does Kamala make after the disappearance of Siddhartha?

    A. She discovers that he caused Kamaswami's business to fail.

    B. She discovers that she is pregnant with his child.

    C. She discovers that he killed the merchant.

    D. She discovers he took all of her money.

7. For what does Siddhartha passionately wish when he leaves Kamala and the town?
   A. Food
   B. Death
   C. Love
   D. Money

8. What sound comes to Siddhartha that awakens his "slumbering soul"?
   A. He hears his father's voice.
   B. He hears, "Om."
   C. He hears his inner self shout, "No!"
   D. He hears the sound of the river.

9. Who does Siddhartha see when he awakes from his long sleep?
   A. Govinda
   B. The Ferryman
   C. Kamala
   D. The Buddha

10. Which is NOT one of the things Siddhartha claims he has had to experience in order to become a child again and begin anew?
    A. Love
    B. Stupidity
    C. Nausea
    D. Disillusionment

Assignment 5
Chapters 9-10

1. What is it that brings Siddhartha feelings of love, enchantment, and gratitude?
    A. His friendship with the Ferryman
    B. His love for the flowing river
    C. His memories of Kamala
    D. His thoughts about his boyhood

2. Who is Vasudeva?
    A. The Buddha
    B. The Ferryman
    C. The merchant
    D. Siddhartha's son

3. What is the first "secret from the river" that Siddhartha learns?
    A. The river holds the voices of everyone in the world.
    B. The river is fluid, like life, ever-changing, ever-moving.
    C. The river is everywhere at the same time, and that the present only exists for it.
    D. The river is the source of all life.

4. What one word does the river pronounce "when one is successful in hearing all its ten thousand voices at the same time"?
    A. Om
    B. Love
    C. Learn
    D. Peace

5. What becomes of Kamala?
    A. She becomes a member of the Buddha's community.
    B. She reveals her love for Siddhartha, and he takes her as his wife.
    C. She is bitten by a snake and dies.
    D. She drowns in the river.

6. How does Siddhartha's son behave while living in the hut by the river?
    A. He honors his father and does what he can to help.
    B. He sulks because he has no one his own age to play with.
    C. He grieves over the loss of his mother and turns to Siddhartha in his pain.
    D. He refuses to do any work and is disrespectful of others.

7. What does Vasudeva suggest Siddhartha should do for his son?
   A. Siddhartha should take the boy back to town to be with people his own age.
   B. Siddhartha should severely punish the boy for his behavior.
   C. Siddhartha should send the boy to the Buddha's community.
   D. Siddhartha should send the boy off to school.

8. What is the boy's reaction when Siddhartha asks him to gather some twigs for the fire?
   A. He does bring back twigs, but he sets the hut on fire out of spite.
   B. He refuses to do the work and runs away the next day.
   C. He does as his father asks but curses his father.
   D. He goes and gets the twigs while planning his revenge.

9. Why does Siddhartha stop looking for his son?
   A. He realizes that he cannot be the father his son wants and deserves.
   B. He realizes it is going to be very difficult to make his son get along with Vasudeva, and he loves Vasudeva more.
   C. He realizes that he cannot help his son and that he shouldn't force himself on him.
   D. He discovers the man he is searching for is not his son.

Assignment 6
Chapters 11-12

1. What knowledge does Siddhartha possess that he many times "doubted...was of such great value?"
    A. He possesses the hope of the river.
    B. He possesses the truth that life is a cyclical path that spirals outward.
    C. He possesses the consciousness of the unity of life.
    D. He possesses the knowledge of what happened to his son.

2. When Siddhartha bends over the water of the river and sees his reflection, of whose face is he reminded?
    A. Govinda's face
    B. The Buddha's face
    C. His father's face
    D. His son's face

3. To what realization does Siddhartha come after seeing his reflection in the water?
    A. He realizes that his father had suffered the same sorrows at Siddhartha's leaving that Siddhartha now suffers at the leaving of his own son.
    B. He realizes how much he truly loved Kamala.
    C. He realizes that he has grown old and has wasted much of his life in sin.
    D. He realizes how he had cheated Kamaswami, and he feels remorse.

4. After listening to the song of the river, where does Vasudeva go?
    A. He goes into the woods to die.
    B. He goes silently to his hut and dies on the same bed as his wife had died.
    C. He leaves in the boat and never returns.
    D. He slips into the river to become one with it as he dies.

5. Who hears tales about the old ferryman by the river and decides to go see him?
    A. Kamaswami
    B. Govinda
    C. The Buddha
    D. Kamala

6. According to Siddhartha, what is the difference between seeking and finding?
    A. Seeking means that one is without love; finding means one has attained it.
    B. Seeking means to have a goal; finding means to be receptive without a goal.
    C. Seeking means to search for knowledge; finding means obtaining it.
    D. Seeking means one is lost; finding means one is found.

7. What does Siddhartha hold in his hand and tell Govinda that it may one day possibly become either a plant, an animal, or a man?
    A. A field mouse
    B. A flower
    C. A grain of rice
    D. A stone

8. What does Govinda claim that the Illustrious One called illusion and forbade his followers to bind themselves?
    A. Lust
    B. Knowledge
    C. Love
    D. Greed

9. What does Govinda see in Siddhartha's face?
    A. He sees the sense of peace that comes from attaining Nirvana.
    B. He sees his own reflection in Siddhartha's eyes.
    C. He sees many other faces all at the same time, and yet they are all Siddhartha.
    D. He sees the pain of the loss of Siddhartha's son and a life ill-spent in sin.

ANSWER KEY: STUDY QUESTIONS *Siddhartha*

	1	2	3	4	5	6
1	D	D	A	A	B	C
2	B	C	D	A	B	C
3	C	D	B	C	C	A
4	B	A	B	D	A	A
5	C	D	A	C	C	B
6	D	D	D	B	D	B
7	A	A	D	B	A	D
8	B	B	D	B	B	C
9	C	D	B	A	C	C
10	B	D	C	A		

VOCABULARY WORKSHEETS

VOCABULARY ASSIGNMENT 1 *Siddhartha*

Part I: Using Prior Knowledge and Contextual Clues

Below are the sentences in which the vocabulary words appear in the text. Read the sentence. Use any clues you can find in the sentence combined with your prior knowledge, and write what you think the underlined words mean on the lines provided.

1. Govinda knew that he would not become an ordinary Brahmin, a lazy sacrificial official, an <u>avaricious</u> dealer in magic sayings, a conceited worthless orator, a wicked sly priest, or just a good stupid sheep amongst a large herd.

    _____

2. Did he not go continually to the holy springs with an <u>insatiable</u> thirst, to the sacrifices, to books, to the Brahmins' discourses?

    _____

3. Wandering <u>ascetics</u>, they were three thin worn-out men, neither old nor young, with dusty and bleeding shoulders, practically naked, scorched by the sun, solitary, strange and hostile--lean jackals in the world of men.

    _____

4. If you find bliss in the forest, come back and teach it to me. If you find <u>disillusionment</u>, come back, and we shall again offer sacrifices to the gods together.

    _____

5. He waited with new thirst like a hunter at a <u>chasm</u> where the life cycle ends, where there is an end to causes, where painless eternity begins.

    _____

6. ... the hour was inevitable when he would again find himself, in sunshine or in moonlight, in shadow or in rain, and was again Self and Siddhartha, again felt the torment of the <u>onerous</u> life cycle.

    _____

7. What is the holding of breath? It is a flight from the Self, it is a temporary escape from the torment of Self. It is a temporary <u>palliative</u> against the pain and folly of life.

    _____

8. "How could it be that amongst so many learned men, amongst so many Brahmins, amongst so many <u>austere</u> and worthy Samanas, amongst so many seekers, so many devoted to inner life, so many holy men, none will find the right way?"

    _____

9. Think, what meaning would our holy prayers have, the <u>venerableness</u> of the Brahmins, the holiness of the Samanas, if, as you say, there is no learning?

    _____

Siddhartha Vocabulary Worksheet Assignment 1 Continued

Part II: Determining the Meaning -- Match the vocabulary words to their dictionary definitions.

____ 1. AVARICIOUS	A. Burdensome; oppressive; troublesome; causing hardship

____ 2. INSATIABLE	B. Immoderately desirous of wealth or gain; greedy

____ 3. ASCETICS	C. Deep cleft in the ground; gorge

____ 4. DISILLUSIONMENT	D. Something that makes pain or sorrow easier to bear

____ 5. CHASM	E. Those who renounce material comforts & lead a life of self-discipline

____ 6. ONEROUS	F. Quality of commanding respect by virtue of age, character, or position

____ 7. PALLIATIVE	G. Incapable of being satisfied or appeased

____ 8. AUSTERE	H. Severe in manner or appearance; strict

____ 9. VENERABLENESS	I. A state of being freed from false beliefs

VOCABULARY ASSIGNMENT 2 *Siddhartha*

Part I: Using Prior Knowledge and Contextual Clues

Below are the sentences in which the vocabulary words appear in the text. Read the sentence. Use any clues you can find in the sentence combined with your prior knowledge, and write what you think the underlined words mean on the lines provided.

1. In the town of Savathi every child knew the name of the illustrious Buddha and every house was ready to fill the <u>alms</u> bowls of Gotama's silently begging disciples.

2. ... and the two Samanas recognized him only by his complete peacefulness of <u>demeanor</u>, by the stillness of his form, in which there was no seeking, no will, no counterfeit, no effort--only light and peace.

3. You have <u>renounced</u> home and parents, you have <u>renounced</u> origin and property, you have <u>renounced</u> your own will, you have <u>renounced</u> friendship.

4. Never has it been presented so clearly, never has it been so <u>irrefutably</u> demonstrated.

5. The Buddha's eyes were lowered, his unfathomable face expressed complete <u>equanimity</u>.

6. Half smiling, with <u>imperturbable</u> brightness and friendliness, the Buddha looked steadily at the stranger and dismissed him with hardly a visible gesture.

7. I will no longer <u>mutilate</u> and destroy myself in order to find a secret behind the ruins.

8. ... it was no longer meaningless and the chance of <u>diversities</u> of the appearances of the world, despised by deep-thinking Brahmins, who scorned diversity, who sought unity.

9. He was no nobleman, belonging to any aristocracy, no <u>artisan</u> belonging to any guild and finding refuge in it, sharing its life and language.

10. He was no nobleman, belonging to any aristocracy, no artisan belonging to any <u>guild</u> and finding refuge in it, sharing its life and language.

Siddhartha Vocabulary Worksheet Assignment 2 Continued

Part II: Determining the Meaning -- Match the vocabulary words to their dictionary definitions.

____ 1. ALMS A. Undeniably; unarguably

____ 2. DEMEANOR B. Gave up or put aside voluntarily

____ 3. RENOUNCED C. Points or aspects in which things differ

____ 4. IRREFUTABLY D. Association of tradesmen

____ 5. EQUANIMITY E. Can't be bothered, agitated, or upset

____ 6. IMPERTURBABLE F. Conduct; behavior; attitude

____ 7. MUTILATE G. Person skilled in an applied art; craftsman

____ 8. DIVERSITIES H. Money, food, or other donations given to the poor

____ 9. ARTISAN I. Injure or disfigure by removing or irreparably damaging parts

____ 10. GUILD J. Quality of being calm and even-tempered; composure

VOCABULARY ASSIGNMENT 3 *Siddhartha*

Part I: Using Prior Knowledge and Contextual Clues
Below are the sentences in which the vocabulary words appear in the text. Read the sentence. Use any clues you can find in the sentence combined with your prior knowledge, and write what you think the underlined words mean on the lines provided.

1. ... but in previous times all this had been nothing to Siddhartha but a fleeting and illusive veil before his eyes, regarded with distrust, condemned to be disregarded and <u>ostracized</u> from the thoughts, because it was not reality, because reality lay on the other side of the visible.

2. No, this world of thought was still on his side, and it led to no goal when one destroyed the senses of the incidental Self but fed it with thoughts and <u>erudition</u>.

3. Then all the magic disappeared from the young woman's smiling face; he saw nothing but the <u>ardent</u> glance of a passionate young woman.

4. He ... learned that it was the grove of Kamala, the well-known <u>courtesan</u>, and that besides the grove she owned a house in the town.

5. Kamaswami is beginning to grow old and <u>indolent</u>. If you please him, he will place great confidence in you.

6. Kamaswami came in, a supple, lively man, with graying hair, with clever, <u>prudent</u> eyes and a sensual mouth.

7. And remembering Kamala's words, [Siddhartha] was never <u>servile</u> to the merchant, but compelled him to treat him as an equal and even more than his equal.

8. "If I ever go there again, ... friendly people will receive me and I will be glad that I did not previously display <u>hastiness</u> and displeasure."

9. He saw them scold and hurt each other; he saw them <u>lament</u> over pains at which the Samana laughs, and suffer at deprivations which a Samana does not feel.

10. You are Kamala and no one else, and within you there is a stillness and <u>sanctuary</u> to which you can retreat at any time and be yourself, just as I can.

Siddhartha Vocabulary Worksheet Assignment 3 Continued

Part II: Determining the Meaning -- Match the vocabulary words to their dictionary definitions.

____ 1. OSTRACIZED   A. Excluded from a group

____ 2. ERUDITION   B. Characteristic of, proper to, or customary for slaves

____ 3. ARDENT   C. Sacred or holy place; place of safety

____ 4. COURTESAN   D. Characterized by intense feeling

____ 5. INDOLENT   E. Feel or express sorrow or regret

____ 6. PRUDENT   F. With overly-eager speed and possible carelessness

____ 7. SERVILE   G. Wise or judicious in practical affairs

____ 8. HASTINESS   H. Inactive; lethargic

____ 9. LAMENT   I. Prostitute or paramour, esp. one associating with noblemen

____ 10. SANCTUARY   J. Knowledge acquired by study; learning

VOCABULARY ASSIGNMENT 4 *Siddhartha*

Part I: Using Prior Knowledge and Contextual Clues

Below are the sentences in which the vocabulary words appear in the text. Read the sentence. Use any clues you can find in the sentence combined with your prior knowledge, and write what you think the underlined words mean on the lines provided.

1. Many of these [things he had learned from the Samanas] he had retained; others were submerged and covered with dust.

   _____

2. Slowly, like moisture entering the dying tree trunk, slowly filling and rotting it, so did the world and inertia creep into Siddhartha's soul; ....

   _____

3. Siddhartha wandered along a strange, twisted path of this last and most base declivity through the game of dice.

   _____

4. Weariness was written on Kamala's beautiful face, ... weariness and incipient old age, and concealed and not yet mentioned, perhaps not yet conscious fear--fear of the autumn of life, fear of old age, fear of death.

   _____

5. Without knowing it, he had endeavored and longed all these years to be like all these other people, ... and yet his life had been much more wretched and poorer than theirs, for their aims were not his, not their sorrows his.

   _____

6. He was full of ennui full of misery, full of death; there was nothing left in the world that could attract him, that could give him pleasure and solace.

   _____

7. "I know you, Govinda, from your father's house and from the Brahmins' school ... and from our sojourn with the Samanas and from that hour in the grove of Jetavana when you swore allegiance to the Illustrious One."

   _____

8. "Remember, my dear Govinda, the world of appearances is transitory, the style of our clothes and hair is extremely transitory."

   _____

9. He had learned these three arts [fasting, waiting, and thinking] and nothing else during the diligent, assiduous years of his youth.

   _____

10. As a young man, I was attracted to expiation. I lived in the woods, suffered heat and cold. I learned to fast, I learned to conquer my body.

    _____

Siddhartha Vocabulary Worksheet Assignment 4 Continued

Part II: Determining the Meaning -- Match the vocabulary words to their dictionary definitions.

____ 1. SUBMERGED   A. Sunk below the surface
____ 2. INERTIA   B. Boredom; dissatisfaction resulting from lack of interest
____ 3. DECLIVITY   C. Downward slope
____ 4. INCIPIENT   D. Beginning to exist or appear
____ 5. WRETCHED   E. Tendency to remain at rest or resist motion or change
____ 6. ENNUI   F. Miserable; very unfortunate
____ 7. SOJOURN   G. Temporary stay; brief period of residence
____ 8. TRANSITORY   H. Act of atoning for sins or wrongdoing
____ 9. ASSIDUOUS   I. Not lasting, permanent, or eternal
____ 10. EXPIATION   J. Constant in effort; working diligently at a task

VOCABULARY ASSIGNMENT 5 *Siddhartha*

Part I: Using Prior Knowledge and Contextual Clues

Below are the sentences in which the vocabulary words appear in the text. Read the sentence. Use any clues you can find in the sentence combined with your prior knowledge, and write what you think the underlined words mean on the lines provided.

1. You have already learned from the river that it is good to <u>strive</u> downwards, to sink, to seek the depths.

   _____

2. I am not a learned man; I do not know how to talk and think. I only know how to listen and be <u>devout</u>; otherwise I have learned nothing.

   _____

3. I have taken thousands of people across and to all of them my river has been nothing but a <u>hindrance</u> on their journey.

   _____

4. As time went on his smile began to resemble the ferryman's, was almost equally radiant, almost equally full of happiness, equally lighting up through a thousand little wrinkles, equally childish, equally <u>senile</u>.

   _____

5. Something <u>emanated</u> from the ferry and from both ferrymen that many of the travelers felt.

   _____

6. Siddhartha treated him with <u>consideration</u> and left him alone, for he respected his grief.

   _____

7. One day, when young Siddhartha was distressing his father with his <u>defiance</u> and temper and had broken both rice bowls, Vasudeva took his friend aside in the evening and talked to him.

   _____

8. Do you not compel this arrogant, spoilt boy to live in a hut with two old banana eaters, to whom even rice is a <u>dainty</u>, whose thoughts cannot be the same as his, ...

   _____

9. He felt a deep love for the runaway boy, like a wound, and yet felt at the same time that this wound was not intended to <u>fester</u> in him, but that it should heal.

   _____

10. And when he felt the wound <u>smarting</u>, he whispered the word Om, filled himself with Om.

    _____

Siddhartha Vocabulary Worksheet Assignment 5 Continued

Part II: Determining the Meaning -- Match the vocabulary words to their dictionary definitions.

____ 1. STRIVE A. Try hard

____ 2. DEVOUT B. Pleasing to the taste, and often temptingly served or delicate

____ 3. HINDRANCE C. Bold resistance to authority or any opposing force

____ 4. SENILE D. Pious; religious; devoted to divine worship or service

____ 5. EMANATED E. Infect, inflame, or corrupt

____ 6. CONSIDERATION F. Hurting with a sharp, usually superficial, stinging pain

____ 7. DEFIANCE G. Of or belonging to old age or aged persons

____ 8. DAINTY H. Thoughtful or sympathetic regard or respect

____ 9. FESTER I. Obstruction; something in the way or a burden

____ 10. SMARTING J. Flowed out from; came from

VOCABULARY ASSIGNMENT 6 *Siddhartha*

Part I: Using Prior Knowledge and Contextual Clues

Below are the sentences in which the vocabulary words appear in the text. Read the sentence. Use any clues you can find in the sentence combined with your prior knowledge, and write what you think the underlined words mean on the lines provided.

1. Their vanities, desires and <u>trivialities</u> no longer seemed absurd to him; they had become understandable, lovable and even worthy of respect.

   _____

2. The men of the world were equal to the thinkers in every other respect and were often superior to them, just as animals in their <u>tenacious</u> undeviating actions in cases of necessity may often seem superior to human beings.

   _____

3. He remembered how once, as a youth, he had <u>compelled</u> his father to let him go and join the ascetics, how he had taken leave of him, how he had gone and never returned.

   _____

4. He mentioned everything, he could tell him everything, even the most painful things; he could <u>disclose</u> everything.

   _____

5. They all belonged to each other: the lament of those who yearn, the laughter of the wise, the cry of <u>indignation</u>, and the groan of the dying.

   _____

6. "But most of all, I have learned from this river and from my <u>predecessor</u>, Vasudeva."

   _____

7. "Wisdom is not <u>communicable</u>. The wisdom which a wise man tries to communicate always sounds foolish."

   _____

8. "During deep meditation, it is possible to <u>dispel</u> time, to see simultaneously all the past, present, and future...."

   _____

9. The river seemed like a god to him and for many years he did not know that every wind, every cloud, every bird, every beetle is equally divine and knows and can teach just as well as the <u>esteemed</u> river.

   _____

10. Govinda said: "But what you call thing, is it something real, something <u>intrinsic</u>? Is it not only the illusion of Maya, only image and appearance?"

    _____

Siddhartha Vocabulary Worksheet Assignment 6 Continued

Part II: Determining the Meaning -- Match the vocabulary words to their dictionary definitions.

____ 1. TRIVIALITIES   A. Anger aroused by something unjust, mean, or unworthy

____ 2. TENACIOUS   B. Make known; reveal; uncover

____ 3. COMPELLED   C. Forced to submit; subdued

____ 4. DISCLOSE   D. Persistent; stubborn

____ 5. INDIGNATION   E. One who came before another in holding an office or position

____ 6. PREDECESSOR   F. Things that are unimportant or frivolous

____ 7. COMMUNICABLE   G. Belonging to a thing by its very nature

____ 8. DISPEL   H. Capable of being easily communicated or transmitted

____ 9. ESTEEMED   I. Respected

____ 10. INTRINSIC   J. Cause to vanish; get rid of

VOCABULARY ANSWER KEY - *Siddhartha*

	1	2	3	4	5	6
1	B	H	A	A	A	F
2	G	F	J	E	D	D
3	E	B	D	C	I	C
4	I	A	I	D	G	B
5	C	J	H	F	J	A
6	A	E	G	B	H	E
7	D	I	B	G	C	H
8	H	C	F	I	B	J
9	F	G	E	J	E	I
10		D	C	H	F	G

DAILY LESSONS

LESSON ONE

Objectives
1. To become familiar with the elements of Joseph Campbell's Hero's Journey
2. To relate the Hero's Journey pattern to three familiar films
3. To introduce Hermann Hesse and his novel *Siddhartha*
4. To preview the study questions and vocabulary for Chapters 1-2
5. To read Chapters 1-2

Activity 1
Ask students to brainstorm what makes a good heroic tale. They should list at least three elements that should be included. Write students' ideas on the board as students share them aloud.

Joseph Campbell, after studying the myths and legends of cultures all over the world, developed what he called The Hero's Journey. The behavioral pattern/growth of the heroes of these myths and legends seemed to form a recurring pattern, which Campbell outlined in his book *The Hero With a Thousand Faces*. The Hero's Journey is almost always a quest for self-knowledge, and Siddhartha goes through his own journey to find just that.

Distribute copies of Steps In The Hero's Journey (master following this lesson). Discuss the steps using the examples given from three films: *The Wizard of Oz*, *Harry Potter and the Sorcerer's Stone*, and *Indiana Jones and the Last Crusade*.

Activity 2
Distribute Writing Assignment #1 and discuss the directions in detail. Explain to students that they will be keeping a journal of personal reflections as they examine their own gaining of self-knowledge. After the entries have been completed, each student will write a poem outlining his/her personal journey. Give students time to write their first journal entries.

Activity 3
Give brief notes about the life of Hermann Hesse (see the introductory materials for this LitPlan), and discuss how certain aspects of his life might have led him to write a book about spiritual growth and the gaining of self-knowledge.

Activity 4
Distribute the materials students will use in this unit. Explain in detail how students are to use these materials.

Study Guides Students should read the study guide questions for each reading assignment prior to beginning the reading assignment to get a feeling for what events and ideas are important in the section they are about to read. After reading the section, students will (as a class or individually) answer the questions to review the important events and ideas from that section of the book. Students should keep the study guides as study materials for the unit test. **Review the study questions for Assignment 1 while you're looking at the study guides.**

Vocabulary Prior to each reading assignment, students will do vocabulary work related to the section of the book they are about to read. Following the completion of the reading of the book, there will be a vocabulary review of all the words used in the vocabulary assignments. Students should keep their vocabulary work as study materials for the unit test. **Do Assignment 1 together orally to show students how to do the vocabulary worksheets.**

Reading Assignment Sheet You need to fill in the reading assignment sheet to let students know by when their reading has to be completed. You can either write the assignment sheet up on a side blackboard or bulletin board and leave it there for students to see each day, or you can make copies for each student to have. In either case, you should advise students to become very familiar with the reading assignments so they know what is expected of them.

Extra Activities Center The Unit Resource Materials portion of this LitPlan contains suggested topics for an extra library of related books and articles in your classroom, as well as crossword and word search puzzles. Make an extra activities center in your room where you will keep these materials for students to use. (Bring the books and articles in from the library and keep several copies of the puzzles on hand.) Explain to students that these materials are available for use when they finish reading assignments or other class work early.

Non-fiction Assignment Sheet Explain to students that they each are to read at least one non-fiction piece at some time during the unit. Students will fill out a Non-fiction Assignment Sheet after completing the reading to help you (the teacher) evaluate their reading experiences and to help the students think about and evaluate their own reading experiences.

Books Each school has its own rules and regulations regarding student use of school books. Advise students of the procedures that are normal for your school. Preview the book. Look at the covers, frontmatter, and index.

Activity 5
Students should read Chapters 1-2 of Siddhartha prior to the next class meeting. If there is time left in this class period, students may begin working on this assignment.

STEPS IN THE HERO'S JOURNEY *Siddhartha*

DEPARTURE

The Call to Adventure
The call to adventure is when something happens or someone arrives in the hero's life that is going to bring about change, whether the hero wants it or not.
    The Wizard of Oz: Miss Gulch arrives to take Toto away from Dorothy.
    Harry Potter: Harry gets a letter in the mail.
    Indiana Jones: Indy receives a package from Venice

Refusal of the Call
The hero often does not believe that he/she (further referenced as "he" for simplicity in writing) is called to do or be something great. He may refuse out of fear or a feeling of inadequacy. Sometimes the hero wishes to go, but outside factors hold him back. If the call is refused, it will return until the hero pays attention and answers.
    The Wizard of Oz: Refusing to accept responsibility for her actions, Dorothy takes Toto and runs away.
    Harry Potter: Uncle Vernon destroys the letters, but they keep coming.
    Indiana Jones: Indy puts the package in his pocket, but when he tries to escape his throng of students, he is abducted by Donovan's men.

Supernatural Aid
The hero may need a bit of nudging to get him to step up to do what needs to be done. At this point, something or someone intervenes to get the hero to pay attention to the call. Often at this step the hero is given a gift or tool that he does not yet know how to use. It is only after facing his trials that he learns its use. (It may also be given during the Initiation Stage by the God/Goddess.)
    The Wizard of Oz: Dorothy runs into a pseudo-fortune teller who encourages her to return home to her aunt.
    Harry Potter: Hagrid arrives at the hut on the rock and says, "Harry, didn't you get my letters?" Hagrid proceeds to ready Harry for his enrollment in Hogwarts, and Harry buys his first wand.
    Indiana Jones: Donovan informs Indy that his father has disappeared and Indy is the only one who can help find both the elder professor and the Holy Grail. Indy realizes that he has received his tool: his father's Grail diary.

The Crossing of the First Threshold
The hero leaves his comfort zone and crosses into the world of the unknown where many lessons await him on the road of trials. It is that first decisive step across that threshold.
    The Wizard of Oz: Dorothy is caught in a twister and whisked away to The Land of Oz.
    Harry Potter: The first time Harry goes to the magical world, it is Hagrid who opens the wall to Diagon Alley. Later Harry crosses the threshold under his own power when finding Platform 9 3/4.
    Indiana Jones: Indy gets on a plane and heads to Venice where his father was last seen.

The Belly of the Whale
This may be categorized as the "put up or shut up" step. The hero has entered an unknown (often dark and mysterious) world, and he must now call upon his resources to continue. If he does not take up the journey, the result may be death (either physical death or death of attaining the goal). By making the decision to follow the path, the hero shows his willingness to undergo a metaphoric death of an old way of thinking or behaving.
    The Wizard of Oz: Dorothy lands in Munchkin Land and must go to the Emerald City if she ever wants to get back home. If not, she will have to take up residence with the Munchkins.

Harry Potter: Harry enters Hogwarts for the first time. If he gives into his fears of inadequacy, he will be forced to return to the Dursleys.
Indiana Jones: Indy picks up the trail where his father was last seen in Venice. He must go down a hole in the floor of the library to find the tomb of Sir Richard, an ancient knight whose shield holds the key to finding the Holy Grail, and hopefully will lead to Indy's lost father.

INITIATION

The Road of Trials
The road of trials is all the obstacles and tests the hero must face as he perseveres towards his goal.
The Wizard of Oz: Dorothy has to go on The Yellow Brick Road, and she has to overcome the obstacles such as the talking trees, the Wicked Witch of the West, the poppies, and the winged monkeys.
Harry Potter: Harry must deal with his classes at Hogwarts, his competitive classmates, etc., as he tries to find his place in the magical world.
Indiana Jones: When Indy finds his father in Vienna, the two of them embark on a quest to find the Holy Grail to keep it out of the hands of the bad guys. They encounter trials on various modes of transportation: car, motorcycle, Zeppelin, tank, horseback, boat, etc.

NOTE: *The next three items are not actual steps in the process (although Joseph Campbell numbers them as such); rather, they are people the hero meets while on his Road of Trials.*

The Meeting With the God or Goddess
The hero meets someone who acts as a mentor/teacher/helper--someone who helps get him started on the Road of Trials.
The Wizard of Oz: Dorothy meets Glinda, the Good Witch of the North. Glinda gives Dorothy the ruby slippers and tells her not to take them off for any reason.
Harry Potter: Harry meets Professor Dumbledore who acts as his strongest mentor.
Indiana Jones: Indy and his father team up against the bad guys; however, not only are they each other's strongest helper (most often by accident), but they actually work against each other because of their bickering.

The Meeting With the Tempter or Temptress
The hero runs into those who prevent him from completing his journey. Sometimes the hero acts as his own worst enemy through self-doubt.
The Wizard of Oz: Dorothy must face the Wicked Witch of the West.
Harry Potter: While his greatest foe is Lord Voldemort, Harry must also deal with Draco Malfoy, Professor Snape, and his own insecurities.
Indiana Jones: Donovan and his cronies try to use Indy and his father to get their hands on the Holy Grail. Indy and his father actually work against each other because of their constant bickering. Elsa Schneider attempts to seduce both Dr. Joneses in order to obtain the Grail diary.

The Companions on the Journey
The hero has someone (or several people) act as companions and friends throughout the journey. Most often, the companions mirror the hero's own talents or weaknesses that he does not recognize in himself.
The Wizard of Oz: Dorothy meets the Scarecrow who wants a brain, which Dorothy certainly wasn't using when she ran away from home, the Tin Man who wants a heart, which Dorothy didn't have when she ran away from home, worrying those who cared for her, and the Cowardly Lion who wants courage, which Dorothy did not have to face problems rather than running away from them.
Harry Potter: Harry meets two friends who suffer from the same sense of insecurity that he feels: Ron Weasley and Hermione Granger.

> **Indiana Jones:** While Indy and his father do have each other, their friend Marcus Brody also appears on the journey.

Atonement With The Father

In this step, the hero must confront his worst inner fears and make peace with himself, peace with the past, or peace with another person in order to continue. It is the sense of inner calm gained from making peace that will give him the added strength needed to accomplish his apotheosis.

> **The Wizard of Oz:** Dorothy sees Aunt Em's face in the crystal ball in the Wicked Witch's dungeon and realizes how badly she hurt her aunt by running away.
>
> **Harry Potter:** Harry sees his family in the Mirror and realizes that they will always be in his life, even if they are not physically with him. After a period of merely sitting in front of the mirror, Dumbledore convinces Harry to live his life and not dwell on the past.
>
> **Indiana Jones:** Each of the Joneses has to make peace with how they have treated the other throughout their lives. When Indy goes over the cliff on the tank, his father finally realizes just how much he has neglected his son. Later, when Indy's father is shot, Indy realizes how much his father means to him, and he risks the challenges in the Cavern of the Crescent Moon in order to save his father's life.

Apotheosis

The apotheosis is the completion of the hero's quest, often after a specific test. The hero faces his foe and proves to himself that he is greater than he ever imagined he could be. Often the hero has finally learned the secret of the tool he was given and is able to use it to complete his apotheosis.

> **The Wizard of Oz:** Dorothy melts the Witch of the West
>
> **Harry Potter:** Harry defeats Voldemort (using his wand).
>
> **Indiana Jones:** Indy passes the tests and obtains the Holy Grail, which saves his father's life (using the Grail diary).

The Ultimate Boon

The ultimate boon is the reward for a job well-done. Sometimes it is not what the hero expected.

> **The Wizard of Oz:** Dorothy gets the broomstick of the Witch of the West. She thinks it will be her key to getting home.
>
> **Harry Potter:** Harry obtains the Sorcerer's Stone and is able to keep it out of the hands of evil.
>
> **Indiana Jones:** Indy and his father get a second chance to build their relationship.

RETURN

Refusal of the Return

Sometimes the hero is content to be where he is, so the hero may hesitate to return home.

> **The Wizard of Oz:** Dorothy hesitates when she cries while telling her friends how much she will miss them.
>
> **Harry Potter:** Harry does not want to go back to the Dursleys.
>
> **Indiana Jones:** The Grail may not be taken from the cavern; it is not meant to be an artifact in a museum.

The Magic Flight

Sometimes the first attempt to go home does not go as well as planned, or it can often be just as difficult as returning from the journey as it was to go on it.

> **The Wizard of Oz:** The balloon leaves without Dorothy.
>
> **Harry Potter:** Harry reluctantly gets on the Hogwarts Express to return to the Dursleys.
>
> **Indiana Jones:** Elsa Schneider tries to take the Grail from the cavern and an earthquake ensues.

Rescue From Without
Just as the hero may need guides and assistants to set out on the quest, often times he must have powerful guides and rescuers to bring him back to everyday life. Often the one who has acted as god or goddess to the hero makes a reappearance.
- **The Wizard of Oz:** Glinda returns and tells Dorothy how to use the ruby slippers.
- **Harry Potter:** Dumbledore assures Harry that he will come back to Hogwarts in the fall.
- **Indiana Jones:** After Indy falls into the abyss trying (unsuccessfully) to save Elsa, Indy's father convinces him to let the Grail go and to take his hand.

The Crossing of the Return Threshold
The hero is finally able to cross that threshold into the "real" world or familiar territory.
- **The Wizard of Oz:** Dorothy clicks her heels and wakes up in her bed in Kansas.
- **Harry Potter:** Harry arrives in London at King's Cross Station.
- **Indiana Jones:** Both Indy and his father escape the collapsing Cavern of the Crescent Moon.

Master of the Two Worlds
While the hero may have returned home (or to a familiar state or a new home), he retains the lessons learned on the journey.
- **The Wizard of Oz:** Dorothy exclaims, "There's no place like home!" which announces her arrival back home and actually states part of what she has learned.
- **Harry Potter:** Harry recognizes that while he must remain at his relatives' home for the summer, he still has the promise of Hogwarts in the fall.
- **Indiana Jones:** Indy and his father retain the lessons learned and rebuild their relationship.

Freedom to Live
The hero is free to live another day and to use his skills learned in future adventures.
- **The Wizard of Oz:** Dorothy claims that the next time she goes looking for her heart's desire, she won't look further than her own back yard.
- **Harry Potter:** Harry will go on to further adventures at Hogwarts and continue in his training.
- **Indiana Jones:** Indy and his father have come to an understanding of one another and will enjoy their new relationship based on what they have learned in their adventure together.

WRITING ASSIGNMENT #1 *Siddhartha*

PROMPT
Webster defines introspection as the "contemplation of one's own thoughts, feelings, and sensations; self-examination." For this series of exercises you will be called upon to examine your own personal Hero's Journey and write journal entries to reflect upon your own strengths and weaknesses as you work to reach your Ultimate Boon and the Freedom to Live, as noted in Campbell's Steps in the Hero's Journey.

Be honest with yourself. These entries will not be collected or read by anyone but YOU; therefore, you will only get out of this exercise what you put into it. All of these entries will be completed in class. After you have completed the journal entries, you will compose a poem that reflects your personal journey towards self-knowledge. The poem will be collected and graded.

PREWRITING
You will be prompted to complete the following journal entries during class time:

Journal Entry One
Fully describe a goal you are working toward. What is the purpose of this goal? What will it help you to achieve after attaining it (your Ultimate Boon)? What strengths do you possess that will help you along the way?

Journal Entry Two
Re-examine your goal. What fears or weaknesses within you (inner obstacles) need to be overcome in order to attain this goal? Do not reflect on outside obstacles. What knowledge or skills do you lack at this point which may hinder your progress if not addressed?

Journal Entry Three
What mentor/helper do you have on your journey to guide you? What skills/talents does this person possess that you would like to acquire within yourself? What tools or gifts have you been given that will help you along the way? What strengths do you have available within you?

Journal Entry Four
What outside obstacles must be faced in order to achieve your goal? How will you successfully overcome these obstacles while still maintaining your true sense of self? How can you honestly bring about change without compromising your own principles or values?

Journal Entry Five
After you have obtained your present goal, what will you do with your new knowledge/skill/gift (Ultimate Boon)? How do you suppose your life will be different after you have succeeded at this task? How may it benefit your life? How might it benefit the lives of others?

Journal Entry Six
Imagine that you have NOT been able to attain your chosen goal. How might this affect your overall journey? What adjustments might need to be made in the event that the original goal set is unobtainable? Will the possibility of falling short of attaining your Ultimate Boon change the way you view yourself or the way you believe others will perceive you? Do you believe that the effort put into the journey will have been wasted? Or do you believe that learning from mistakes/failure is a part of the learning process? Explain your answer in depth.

DRAFTING
Your poem will be a narrative poem (a short story in poetic form) that outlines your personal journey towards your chosen goal. Be sure to include the use of the poet's tools (such as

symbolism, metaphor, imagery, simile, or personification, as well as the use of rhyme and meter) and incorporate at least six vocabulary words into your poem.

REVISING
When you finish the rough draft of your poem, ask a student who sits near you to read it. After reading your rough draft, he/she should tell you what he/she liked best about your work, which parts were difficult to understand, and ways in which your work could be improved. Re-read your poem considering your critic's comments and make the corrections you feel are necessary.

PROOFREADING
Do a final proofreading of your poem, double-checking your spelling and other conventions of writing.

REMEMBER: It's the journey, not the destination that is important!

LESSON TWO

Objectives

1. To review the main events and ideas from Chapters 1-2
2. To demonstrate reading comprehension through sharing responses to study guide questions
3. To demonstrate understanding of characterization
4. To improve cooperative learning skills through working in groups
5. To demonstrate comprehension of Joseph Campbell's Hero's Journey pattern through outlining the Departure Stage for *Siddhartha*
6. To improve speaking skills through the presentation of information
7. To practice note-taking skills through listening to presentations
8. To preview the study questions and vocabulary for Chapters 3-4
9. To read Chapters 3-4

Activity 1
Give students a few minutes to formulate answers for the study guide questions for Chapters 1-2, then discuss the answers to the questions in detail. Write the answers on the board or overhead transparency so students can have the correct answers for study purposes.

NOTE: It is a good practice in public speaking and leadership skills for individual students to take charge of leading the discussions of the study questions. Perhaps a different student could go to the front of the class and lead the discussion each day that the study questions are discussed in this unit. Of course, you should guide the discussion when appropriate and try to fill in any gaps students may leave. The study questions could really be handled in a number of different ways, including in small groups with group reports following. Occasionally you may want to use the multiple choice questions as quizzes to check students' reading comprehension. As a short review now and then, students could pair up for the first (or last, if you have time left at the end of a class period) few minutes of class to quiz each other from the study questions. Mix up methods of reviewing the materials and checking comprehension throughout the unit so students don't get bored just answering the questions the same way each day. Variety in methods will also help address the different learning styles of your students. From now on in this unit, the directions will simply say, "Discuss the answers to the study questions in detail as previously directed." You will choose the method of preparation and discussion each day based on what best suits you and your class.

Activity 2
Give students time to write Journal Entry Two.

Activity 3
Separate the class into five groups and assign each group one of the following: Siddhartha's Positive Traits, Siddhartha's Negative Traits, Govinda, Siddhartha's father, and the Samanas. Each group is to identify three character traits and support their choices with evidence from the text.

When the groups are finished, have each group share its findings and make connections between characters. How do they relate to each other?

Activity 4
Keeping the same five groups, assign each group one of the steps in the Departure Stage from Joseph Campbell's Hero's Journey: The Call to Adventure, The Refusal of the Call, Supernatural

Aid, Crossing the First Threshold, and The Belly of the Whale. Have each group identify the step of the journey for Siddhartha and draw a poster depicting the step. Have each group select a quotation from the novel to act as a caption for their drawings.

Going in order, have the groups outline the Departure Stage for Siddhartha. While each group shares, those listening should take notes so that everyone will have an outline in progress of Siddhartha's journey. Create a Hero's Journey bulletin board using the posters students make.

Activity 5
Remind students to preview the study questions, do the vocabulary work for Chapters 3-4 and read those chapters prior to the next class.

LESSON THREE

Objectives
1. To review the main events and ideas of Chapters 3-4
2. To demonstrate reading comprehension through taking a quiz
3. To read non-fiction articles relating to the historical Siddhartha Gautama
4. To practice research skills in the library/media center
5. To preview the study questions and vocabulary for Chapters 5-6
6. To read Chapters 5-6

Activity 1
Discuss the answers for the study questions for Chapters 3-4 as previously directed.

Activity 2
Distribute the quizzes for Chapters 1-4. Give students ample time to complete them then discuss the answers, checking the papers orally in class. Collect for recording grades, if desired.

Activity 3
Students will use this time to write journal entry #3.

Activity 4
Take students to the library/media center (unless you want them to do the non-fiction assignment independently). Distribute the Non-fiction Assignment sheets. Explain that students will choose a topic related to the book, find articles relating to that topic, and report about the article of their choice on the Non-fiction Assignment Sheet. Tell students when these will be collected.

Activity 5
Remind students to preview the study questions and do the vocabulary work for Chapters 5-6 and then read those chapters prior to the next class meeting.

Siddhartha QUIZ CHAPTERS 1-4

I. Multiple Choice Chapters 1-4

1. What has caused Siddhartha "to feel the seeds of discontent within him"?
   A. Siddhartha cannot find his one true love.
   B. Siddhartha desires to travel to see far away lands.
   C. Siddhartha wishes to attend a university.
   D. Siddhartha believes that he has obtained all the knowledge that his father and teachers can offer, but it is not enough.

2. After Siddhartha decides not to join the Buddha's community, from whom does he choose to learn?
   A. He chooses to learn from the university.
   B. He chooses to learn from Govinda.
   C. He chooses to learn from his father.
   D. He chooses to learn from himself.

3. What realization gives Siddhartha the feeling of awakening from a long dream?
   A. He realizes he has been afraid of being himself, and so he has tried to lose himself in the teachings of others.
   B. He realizes how foolish the Buddha's teaching are.
   C. After meeting women, he realizes what he has missed by denying his senses.
   D. He realizes that he needs to return home to ask for his father's forgiveness.

4. What separates Govinda and Siddhartha?
   A. Govinda joins the Buddha's community.
   B. Siddhartha returns to his home village.
   C. Govinda is discouraged and leaves the Samanas for a life of the senses.
   D. Siddhartha is bitten by a poisonous snake and dies.

5. Why is Siddhartha not very curious about the teachings of the Buddha?
   A. He does not agree with what the Buddha teaches.
   B. Since the Buddha is not a Samana, Siddhartha does not care to listen to him.
   C. Siddhartha has not heard of the Buddha.
   D. He does not think the Buddha can teach him anything new.

6. What is Jetavana?
   A. It is a trance-like state of euphoria.
   B. It is the name of the town where Siddhartha grew up.
   C. It is the Buddha's favorite place to stay.
   D. It is a prayer recited by the Samanas each evening.

7. How does Siddhartha prove that he has mastered all that the Samana can teach him?
   A. Siddhartha reads the old man's mind.
   B. Siddhartha hypnotizes the eldest Samana.
   C. Siddhartha prays and makes it rain.
   D. Siddhartha fasts for seven days.

8. Which is NOT a change that takes place in Siddhartha while on the road with the Samanas?
   A. He looks at well-dressed people with contempt.
   B. He snarls at women.
   C. His nails grow long.
   D. He becomes fat from over-indulging in food.

9. Who accompanies Siddhartha on his journey to become a Samana?
   A. Siddhartha's father accompanies with him.
   B. Siddhartha's younger brother accompanies with him.
   C. Siddhartha's future bride accompanies with him.
   D. Govinda accompanies Siddhartha.

10. After Siddhartha leaves Jetavana grove, where does he initially intend to go?
    A. He intends to go home to see his father.
    B. He intends to go seek peace in the mountains.
    C. He intends to find a wife.
    D. He intends to follow the Buddha.

II. Vocabulary Chapters 1-4

____ 1. AVARICIOUS   A. Burdensome; oppressive; troublesome; causing hardship

____ 2. INSATIABLE   B. Gave up or put aside voluntarily

____ 3. CHASM   C. Quality of being calm and even-tempered; composure

____ 4. ONEROUS   D. Deep cleft in the ground; gorge

____ 5. AUSTERE   E. Incapable of being satisfied or appeased

____ 6. DEMEANOR   F. Severe in manner or appearance; strict

____ 7. RENOUNCED   G. Immoderately desirous of wealth or gain; greedy

____ 8. EQUANIMITY   H. Person skilled in an applied art; craftsman

____ 9. MUTILATE   I. Conduct; behavior; attitude

____ 10. ARTISAN   J. Injure or disfigure by removing or irreparably damaging parts

Siddhartha QUIZ CHAPTERS 1-4 Answer Key

I. Multiple Choice Chapters 1-4

D 1. What has caused Siddhartha "to feel the seeds of discontent within him"?
- A. Siddhartha cannot find his one true love.
- B. Siddhartha desires to travel to see far away lands.
- C. Siddhartha wishes to attend a university.
- D. Siddhartha believes that he has obtained all the knowledge that his father and teachers can offer, but it is not enough.

D 2. After Siddhartha decides not to join the Buddha's community, from whom does he choose to learn?
- A. He chooses to learn from the university.
- B. He chooses to learn from Govinda.
- C. He chooses to learn from his father.
- D. He chooses to learn from himself.

A 3. What realization gives Siddhartha the feeling of awakening from a long dream?
- A. He realizes he has been afraid of being himself, and so he has tried to lose himself in the teachings of others.
- B. He realizes how foolish the Buddha's teaching are.
- C. After meeting women, he realizes what he has missed by denying his senses.
- D. He realizes that he needs to return home to ask for his father's forgiveness.

A 4. What separates Govinda and Siddhartha?
- A. Govinda joins the Buddha's community.
- B. Siddhartha returns to his home village.
- C. Govinda is discouraged and leaves the Samanas for a life of the senses.
- D. Siddhartha is bitten by a poisonous snake and dies.

D 5. Why is Siddhartha not very curious about the teachings of the Buddha?
- A. He does not agree with what the Buddha teaches.
- B. Since the Buddha is not a Samana, Siddhartha does not care to listen to him.
- C. Siddhartha has not heard of the Buddha.
- D. He does not think the Buddha can teach him anything new.

C 6. What is Jetavana?
- A. It is a trance-like state of euphoria.
- B. It is the name of the town where Siddhartha grew up.
- C. It is the Buddha's favorite place to stay.
- D. It is a prayer recited by the Samanas each evening.

B 7. How does Siddhartha prove that he has mastered all that the Samana can teach him?
- A. Siddhartha reads the old man's mind.
- B. Siddhartha hypnotizes the eldest Samana.
- C. Siddhartha prays and makes it rain.
- D. Siddhartha fasts for seven days.

D 8. Which is NOT a change that takes place in Siddhartha while on the road with the Samanas?
- A. He looks at well-dressed people with contempt.
- B. He snarls at women.
- C. His nails grow long.
- D. He becomes fat from over-indulging in food.

D 9. Who accompanies Siddhartha on his journey to become a Samana?
- A. Siddhartha's father accompanies with him.
- B. Siddhartha's younger brother accompanies with him.
- C. Siddhartha's future bride accompanies with him.
- D. Govinda accompanies Siddhartha.

A 10. After Siddhartha leaves Jetavana grove, where does he initially intend to go?
- A. He intends to go home to see his father.
- B. He intends to go seek peace in the mountains.
- C. He intends to find a wife.
- D. He intends to follow the Buddha.

II. Vocabulary Chapters 1-4

G	1.	AVARICIOUS	A.	Burdensome; oppressive; troublesome; causing hardship
E	2.	INSATIABLE	B.	Gave up or put aside voluntarily
D	3.	CHASM	C.	Quality of being calm and even-tempered; composure
A	4.	ONEROUS	D.	Deep cleft in the ground; gorge
F	5.	AUSTERE	E.	Incapable of being satisfied or appeased
I	6.	DEMEANOR	F.	Severe in manner or appearance; strict
B	7.	RENOUNCED	G.	Immoderately desirous of wealth or gain; greedy
C	8.	EQUANIMITY	H.	Person skilled in an applied art; craftsman
J	9.	MUTILATE	I.	Conduct; behavior; attitude
H	10.	ARTISAN	J.	Injure or disfigure by removing or irreparably damaging parts

NON-FICTION READING ASSIGNMENT *Siddhartha*

Your task is to research a topic related to *Siddhartha*. Choose one of the topics below (or if there is a different topic you want to explore, get approval for that topic), read a long article or a couple of shorter ones about that topic, and report your findings on the form provided.

You will also be reporting the information with your classmates, so be prepared to give a short oral report.

Suggested topics:

Background of Siddhartha Gautama's time period and geographic location
Summary of Siddhartha Gautama's life
The Four Noble Truths
The Eightfold Noble Path
Bodhi Tree
Basic Beliefs and Practices of Buddhism
Jhana
Karma
Nirvana
Dhamma
Parinibbana
Reincarnation
Caste System
Nepal
East Indian Culture
Herman Hesse
Buddhism in the Modern World
Brahmin
Ascetism

NON-FICTION ASSIGNMENT SHEET
(To be completed after reading the required nonfiction article)

Name _____ Date _____

Title of Nonfiction Read _____

Written By _____ Publication Date _____

I. Factual Summary—Write a short summary of the piece you read.

II. Vocabulary
   1. With which vocabulary words in the piece did you encounter some degree of difficulty?

   2. How did you resolve your lack of understanding with these words?

III. Interpretation: What was the main point the author wanted you to get from reading his work?

IV. Criticism
   1. With which points of the piece did you agree or find easy to accept? Why?

   2. With which points of the piece did you disagree or find difficult to believe? Why?

V. Personal Response: What do you think about this piece? OR How does this piece influence your ideas?

69

LESSON FOUR

Objectives
1. To review the main events and ideas from Chapters 5-6
2. To practice oral reading skills
3. To preview the study questions and vocabulary for Chapters 7-8
4. To read Chapters 7-8

Activity 1
Discuss the answers to the study questions for Chapters 5-6 as previously directed.

While students have their study guides out, preview the study questions for Chapters 7-8.

Activity 2
Give students ample time to complete journal entry #4.

Activity 3
Take a few minutes to review the vocabulary work from Chapters 5-6 and do the work for Chapters 7-8 together orally in class.

Activity 4
Have students read Chapters 7-8 of Siddhartha orally in class. You know the best way to get readers with your class: pick students at random, ask for volunteers, or use whatever method works best for your class. If you have not yet completed an oral reading evaluation this marking period, this would be a good opportunity to do so. A form is included for your convenience.

If you do not complete reading these chapters in class, students should do so prior to the next class meeting.

If you do not complete the oral reading evaluations, use another class period for oral reading to finish the evaluations.

ORAL READING EVALUATION *Siddhartha*

Name _____ Class _____ Date _____

SKILL	EXCELLENT	GOOD	AVERAGE	FAIR	POOR
Fluency	5	4	3	2	1
Clarity	5	4	3	2	1
Audibility	5	4	3	2	1
Pronunciation	5	4	3	2	1
_____	5	4	3	2	1
_____	5	4	3	2	1

Total _____   Grade _____

Comments:

LESSON FIVE

Objectives
1. To review the main events and ideas of Chapters 7-8
2. To demonstrate reading comprehension through taking a quiz
3. To check students' non-fiction reading assignments
4. To practice public speaking skills
5. To work in cooperative groups
6. To preview the study questions and vocabulary for Chapters 9-10
7. To read Chapters 9-10

Activity 1
Discuss the study questions for Chapters 7-8 as previously directed.

While students have their study guides out, preview the study questions for Chapters 9-10.

You might also want to take this time to review the vocabulary answers for Chapters 7-8.

Activity 2
Distribute quizzes for Chapters 5-8. Give students ample time to complete them, then grade them orally in class. Collect them for recording grades, if desired.

Activity 3
Give students time to complete journal entry #5.

Activity 4
Have students share the information they found doing their non-fiction reading assignments. Each student should give an oral report summarizing the information he/she read. It can be helpful to have students who did the same topics report back-to-back. The reports do not have to be long; just a short summary.

Activity 5
Divide the class into eight groups, one for each of the items in the Eightfold Noble Path.

1. right understanding
2. right thought
3. right speech
4. right action
5. right livelihood
6. right effort
7. right mindfulness
8. right concentration

Each group is to discuss the meaning of that portion of the Eightfold Noble Path and why it was important to the teachings of Siddhartha Gautama. Each group will come up with an example of how one can live that portion of the Eightfold Noble Path.

Option: Groups may each create a poster depicting the example they choose. Then, use the posters to create a display or bulletin board about the Eightfold Noble Path.

When their group discussions are completed, have each group report to the class.

Activity 6
Remind students that they should do the vocabulary work for Chapters 9-10, then read those chapters prior to the next class.

Siddhartha QUIZ CHAPTERS 5-8

I. Multiple Choice Chapters 5-8

1. When Siddhartha decides to be "present" in the world, what does he begin to notice about it?
    A. He notices the ugliness of what man has done to nature.
    B. He notices how large the world really is outside of his little village.
    C. He notices how petty people act towards each other.
    D. He notices the beauty of nature that he had never paid attention to before.

2. Who is Kamala?
    A. Kamala is the real name of the Buddha.
    B. Kamala is a rich merchant who teaches Siddhartha about business.
    C. Kamala is a ferryman who tells Siddhartha secrets of the river.
    D. Kamala is a beautiful courtesan who teaches Siddhartha about love.

3. Who is Kamaswami?
    A. Kamaswami is a rich merchant.
    B. Kamaswami is the real name of the Buddha.
    C. Kamaswami is a ferryman.
    D. Kamaswami is a courtesan.

4. What is Siddhartha's attitude toward business?
    A. Siddhartha is more concerned about doing the right thing and helping others than making a profit.
    B. Siddhartha is indifferent towards business and unconcerned about making a profit.
    C. Siddhartha thinks business is bad for the soul.
    D. Siddhartha meticulous in his business dealings and accounting.

5. To what does Siddhartha compare those who have no "stillness and sanctuary to which [they] can retreat at any time"?
   A. He compares them to falling leaves that have no direction.
   B. He compares them to the flowing river.
   C. He compares them to a snake shedding its skin.
   D. He compares them to a heron flying high in the sky.

6. When Siddhartha's soul goes to sleep, what becomes more awakened?
   A. His senses
   B. His intellect
   C. His consciousness
   D. His enlightenment

7. What does Siddhartha dream when he becomes dissatisfied with his gambling life?
   A. He dreams that he becomes the Buddha and lives a life of peace.
   B. He dreams that his father is displeased with him and dies of a broken heart.
   C. He dreams that Kamala's bird dies in its cage, and he throws it away on the road.
   D. He dreams that Govinda becomes a woman, and he is attracted to him.

8. For what does Siddhartha passionately wish when he leaves Kamala and the town?
   A. Money
   B. Love
   C. Food
   D. Death

9. Who does Siddhartha see when he awakes from his long sleep?
   A. The Ferryman
   B. Kamala
   C. Govinda
   D. The Buddha

10. Which is NOT one of the things Siddhartha claims he has had to experience in order to become a child again and begin anew?
    A. Disillusionment
    B. Stupidity
    C. Nausea
    D. Love

II. Vocabulary Chapters 5-8

____ 1. OSTRACIZED   A. Excluded from a group
____ 2. ERUDITION   B. Wise or judicious in practical affairs
____ 3. INDOLENT   C. Downward slope
____ 4. PRUDENT   D. Act of atoning for sins or wrongdoing
____ 5. LAMENT   E. Feel or express sorrow or regret
____ 6. INERTIA   F. Knowledge acquired by study; learning
____ 7. DECLIVITY   G. Tendency to remain at rest or resist motion or change
____ 8. ENNUI   H. Boredom; dissatisfaction resulting from lack of interest
____ 9. ASSIDUOUS   I. Constant in effort; working diligently at a task
____ 10. EXPIATION   J. Inactive; lethargic

Siddhartha QUIZ CHAPTERS 5-8 Answer Key

I. Multiple Choice Chapters 5-8

D 1. When Siddhartha decides to be "present" in the world, what does he begin to notice about it?
- A. He notices the ugliness of what man has done to nature.
- B. He notices how large the world really is outside of his little village.
- C. He notices how petty people act towards each other.
- D. He notices the beauty of nature that he had never paid attention to before.

D 2. Who is Kamala?
- A. Kamala is the real name of the Buddha.
- B. Kamala is a rich merchant who teaches Siddhartha about business.
- C. Kamala is a ferryman who tells Siddhartha secrets of the river.
- D. Kamala is a beautiful courtesan who teaches Siddhartha about love.

A 3. Who is Kamaswami?
- A. Kamaswami is a rich merchant.
- B. Kamaswami is the real name of the Buddha.
- C. Kamaswami is a ferryman.
- D. Kamaswami is a courtesan.

B 4. What is Siddhartha's attitude toward business?
- A. Siddhartha is more concerned about doing the right thing and helping others than making a profit.
- B. Siddhartha is indifferent towards business and unconcerned about making a profit.
- C. Siddhartha thinks business is bad for the soul.
- D. Siddhartha meticulous in his business dealings and accounting.

A 5. To what does Siddhartha compare those who have no "stillness and sanctuary to which [they] can retreat at any time"?
- A. He compares them to falling leaves that have no direction.
- B. He compares them to the flowing river.
- C. He compares them to a snake shedding its skin.
- D. He compares them to a heron flying high in the sky.

A 6. When Siddhartha's soul goes to sleep, what becomes more awakened?
- A. His senses
- B. His intellect
- C. His consciousness
- D. His enlightenment

C 7. What does Siddhartha dream when he becomes dissatisfied with his gambling life?
- A. He dreams that he becomes the Buddha and lives a life of peace.
- B. He dreams that his father is displeased with him and dies of a broken heart.
- C. He dreams that Kamala's bird dies in its cage, and he throws it away on the road.
- D. He dreams that Govinda becomes a woman, and he is attracted to him.

D 8. For what does Siddhartha passionately wish when he leaves Kamala and the town?
- A. Money
- B. Love
- C. Food
- D. Death

C 9. Who does Siddhartha see when he awakes from his long sleep?
- A. The Ferryman
- B. Kamala
- C. Govinda
- D. The Buddha

D 10. Which is NOT one of the things Siddhartha claims he has had to experience in order to become a child again and begin anew?
- A. Disillusionment
- B. Stupidity
- C. Nausea
- D. Love

II. Vocabulary Chapters 5-8

A	1.	OSTRACIZED	A.	Excluded from a group
F	2.	ERUDITION	B.	Wise or judicious in practical affairs
J	3.	INDOLENT	C.	Downward slope
B	4.	PRUDENT	D.	Act of atoning for sins or wrongdoing
E	5.	LAMENT	E.	Feel or express sorrow or regret
G	6.	INERTIA	F.	Knowledge acquired by study; learning
C	7.	DECLIVITY	G.	Tendency to remain at rest or resist motion or change
H	8.	ENNUI	H.	Boredom; dissatisfaction resulting from lack of interest
I	9.	ASSIDUOUS	I.	Constant in effort; working diligently at a task
D	10.	EXPIATION	J.	Inactive; lethargic

LESSON SIX

Objectives
1. To review the main ideas and events of Chapters 9-10
2. To demonstrate comprehension of the second stage of Joseph Campbell's Hero's Journey: The Initiation
3. To demonstrate cooperative skills through group work
4. To practice public speaking through oral presentations
5. To practice note-taking skills
6. To preview the study questions and vocabulary for Chapters 11-12
7. To read chapters 11-12

Activity 1
Discuss the answers to the study questions for Chapters 9-10 as previously directed.

While students have their study guides out, preview the questions for Chapters 11-12.

You may also want to discuss the correct answers to the vocabulary worksheet for Chapters 9-10 at this time.

Activity 2
Give students time to complete journal entry #6.

Activity 3
Break the class into nine groups or pairs (mixing students up from previous group work). Today the groups will focus on Siddhartha's Road of Trials and those he met along the way. Each chapter (2-10) is a portion of Siddhartha's Initiation Stage.

Group Chapter Assignments:
With the Samana	Samsara
Gotama	By the River
Awakening	The Ferryman
Kamala	The Son
Amongst the People	

Each group will answer the following questions (write them where all students can see and/or copy them):

1. What trial does Siddhartha have to overcome in this chapter?
2. What does he learn about himself or about the world?
3. Who helps him through this ordeal?
4. Who hinders his progress? How does Siddhartha deal with this?

Have each group create a poster depicting Siddhartha's Road of Trials to be added to the Hero's Journey bulletin board.

Activity 4
Remind students to do the vocabulary work for Chapters 11-12 and then to read those chapters prior to your next class meeting.

LESSON SEVEN

Objectives
1. To review the main events and ideas of Chapters 11-12
2. To demonstrate reading comprehension through a quiz
3. To demonstrate comprehension of the remaining steps of Joseph Campbell's Hero's Journey
4. To begin creating a narrative poem about students' personal journeys

Activity 1
Discuss the answers to the study questions for Chapters 11-12 as previously directed.

Discuss the answers to the vocabulary worksheet for Chapters 11-12.

Activity 2
Distribute the quizzes for Chapters 9-12. Give students ample time to complete them, then discuss the answers orally in class. Collect the quizzes to record the grades (optional).

Activity 3
As a class, discuss the remaining steps of the Initiation Stage (Atonement with the Father, Apotheosis, and Ultimate Boon) as well as the Return Stage for Siddhartha. Each student should add the steps to their notes about Siddhartha's Hero's Journey. What elements of self-knowledge does Siddhartha gain as a result of this journey?

Activity 4
If time remains in this class period, give students time to read through their journal entries and begin plotting out their narrative poems (Writing Assignment #1). Explain that a narrative poem is a short story in poetic form.)

Siddhartha QUIZ CHAPTERS 9-12

I. Multiple Choice Chapters 9-12

1. Who is Vasudeva?
   A. The merchant
   B. The Ferryman
   C. The Buddha
   D. Siddhartha's son

2. What does Govinda claim that the Illustrious One called illusion and forbade his followers to bind themselves?
   A. Love
   B. Greed
   C. Lust
   D. Knowledge

3. According to Siddhartha, what is the difference between seeking and finding?
   A. Seeking means that one is without love; finding means one has attained it.
   B. Seeking means one is lost; finding means one is found.
   C. Seeking means to have a goal; finding means to be receptive without a goal.
   D. Seeking means to search for knowledge; finding means obtaining it.

4. After listening to the song of the river, where does Vasudeva go?
   A. He goes into the woods to die.
   B. He goes silently to his hut and dies on the same bed as his wife had died.
   C. He leaves in the boat and never returns.
   D. He slips into the river to become one with it as he dies.

5. To what realization does Siddhartha come after seeing his reflection in the water?
   A. He realizes how he had cheated Kamaswami, and he feels remorse.
   B. He realizes that his father had suffered the same sorrows at Siddhartha's leaving that Siddhartha now suffers at the leaving of his own son.
   C. He realizes that he has grown old and has wasted much of his life in sin.
   D. He realizes how much he truly loved Kamala.

6. Why does Siddhartha stop looking for his son?
    A. He realizes it is going to be very difficult to make his son get along with Vasudeva, and he loves Vasudeva more.
    B. He discovers the man he is searching for is not his son.
    C. He realizes that he cannot be the father his son wants and deserves.
    D. He realizes that he cannot help his son and that he shouldn't force himself on him.

7. How does Siddhartha's son behave while living in the hut by the river?
    A. He refuses to do any work and is disrespectful of others.
    B. He grieves over the loss of his mother and turns to Siddhartha in his pain.
    C. He honors his father and does what he can to help.
    D. He sulks because he has no one his own age to play with.

8. What becomes of Kamala?
    A. She is bitten by a snake and dies.
    B. She reveals her love for Siddhartha, and he takes her as his wife.
    C. She drowns in the river.
    D. She becomes a member of the Buddha's community.

9. What is the first "secret from the river" that Siddhartha learns?
    A. The river holds the voices of everyone in the world.
    B. The river is everywhere at the same time, and that the present only exists for it.
    C. The river is the source of all life.
    D. The river is fluid, like life, ever-changing, ever-moving.

10. What does Govinda see in Siddhartha's face?
    A. He sees the sense of peace that comes from attaining Nirvana.
    B. He sees the pain of the loss of Siddhartha's son and a life ill-spent in sin.
    C. He sees many other faces all at the same time, and yet they are all Siddhartha.
    D. He sees his own reflection in Siddhartha's eyes.

II. Vocabulary Chapters 9-12

____ 1. DEVOUT   A. Make known; reveal; uncover

____ 2. SENILE   B. Pleasing to the taste, and often temptingly served or delicate

____ 3. EMANATED   C. Pious; religious; devoted to divine worship or service

____ 4. DAINTY   D. Capable of being easily communicated or transmitted

____ 5. FESTER   E. Of or belonging to old age or aged persons

____ 6. TENACIOUS   F. Belonging to a thing by its very nature

____ 7. DISCLOSE   G. Infect, inflame, or corrupt

____ 8. COMMUNICABLE   H. Cause to vanish; get rid of

____ 9. DISPEL   I. Persistent; stubborn

____ 10. INTRINSIC   J. Flowed out from; came from

Siddhartha QUIZ CHAPTERS 9-12 Answer Key

I. Multiple Choice Chapters 9-12

B 1. Who is Vasudeva?
- A. The merchant
- B. The Ferryman
- C. The Buddha
- D. Siddhartha's son

A 2. What does Govinda claim that the Illustrious One called illusion and forbade his followers to bind themselves?
- A. Love
- B. Greed
- C. Lust
- D. Knowledge

C 3. According to Siddhartha, what is the difference between seeking and finding?
- A. Seeking means that one is without love; finding means one has attained it.
- B. Seeking means one is lost; finding means one is found.
- C. Seeking means to have a goal; finding means to be receptive without a goal.
- D. Seeking means to search for knowledge; finding means obtaining it.

A 4. After listening to the song of the river, where does Vasudeva go?
- A. He goes into the woods to die.
- B. He goes silently to his hut and dies on the same bed as his wife had died.
- C. He leaves in the boat and never returns.
- D. He slips into the river to become one with it as he dies.

B 5. To what realization does Siddhartha come after seeing his reflection in the water?
- A. He realizes how he had cheated Kamaswami, and he feels remorse.
- B. He realizes that his father had suffered the same sorrows at Siddhartha's leaving that Siddhartha now suffers at the leaving of his own son.
- C. He realizes that he has grown old and has wasted much of his life in sin.
- D. He realizes how much he truly loved Kamala.

D 6. Why does Siddhartha stop looking for his son?
- A. He realizes it is going to be very difficult to make his son get along with Vasudeva, and he loves Vasudeva more.
- B. He discovers the man he is searching for is not his son.
- C. He realizes that he cannot be the father his son wants and deserves.
- D. He realizes that he cannot help his son and that he shouldn't force himself on him.

A 7. How does Siddhartha's son behave while living in the hut by the river?
- A. He refuses to do any work and is disrespectful of others.
- B. He grieves over the loss of his mother and turns to Siddhartha in his pain.
- C. He honors his father and does what he can to help.
- D. He sulks because he has no one his own age to play with.

A 8. What becomes of Kamala?
- A. She is bitten by a snake and dies.
- B. She reveals her love for Siddhartha, and he takes her as his wife.
- C. She drowns in the river.
- D. She becomes a member of the Buddha's community.

B 9. What is the first "secret from the river" that Siddhartha learns?
- A. The river holds the voices of everyone in the world.
- B. The river is everywhere at the same time, and that the present only exists for it.
- C. The river is the source of all life.
- D. The river is fluid, like life, ever-changing, ever-moving.

C 10. What does Govinda see in Siddhartha's face?
- A. He sees the sense of peace that comes from attaining Nirvana.
- B. He sees the pain of the loss of Siddhartha's son and a life ill-spent in sin.
- C. He sees many other faces all at the same time, and yet they are all Siddhartha.
- D. He sees his own reflection in Siddhartha's eyes.

II. Vocabulary Chapters 9-12

C	1.	DEVOUT	A.	Make known; reveal; uncover
E	2.	SENILE	B.	Pleasing to the taste, and often temptingly served or delicate
J	3.	EMANATED	C.	Pious; religious; devoted to divine worship or service
B	4.	DAINTY	D.	Capable of being easily communicated or transmitted
G	5.	FESTER	E.	Of or belonging to old age or aged persons
I	6.	TENACIOUS	F.	Belonging to a thing by its very nature
A	7.	DISCLOSE	G.	Infect, inflame, or corrupt
D	8.	COMMUNICABLE	H.	Cause to vanish; get rid of
H	9.	DISPEL	I.	Persistent; stubborn
F	10.	INTRINSIC	J.	Flowed out from; came from

LESSON EIGHT

<u>Objectives</u>
　　　　To review all of the vocabulary work done in the unit

<u>Activity</u>
Choose one (or more) of the vocabulary review activities listed below and spend your class period as directed in the activity. Some of the materials for these review activities are located in the Vocabulary Resource Materials section in this LitPlan.

VOCABULARY REVIEW ACTIVITIES

1. Divide your class into two teams and have an old-fashioned spelling or definition bee.

2. Give each of your students (or students in groups of two, three or four) a *Siddhartha* Vocabulary Word Search Puzzle. The person (group) to find all of the vocabulary words in the puzzle first wins.

3. Give students a *Siddhartha* Vocabulary Word Search Puzzle without the word list. The person or group to find the most vocabulary words in the puzzle wins.

4. Use a *Siddhartha* Vocabulary Crossword Puzzle. Put the puzzle onto a transparency on the overhead projector (so everyone can see it), and do the puzzle together as a class.

5. Give students a *Siddhartha* Vocabulary Matching Worksheet to do.

6. Divide your class into two teams. Use *Siddhartha* vocabulary words with their letters jumbled as a word list. Student 1 from Team A faces off against Student 1 from Team B. You write the first jumbled word on the board. The first student (1A or 1B) to unscramble the word wins the chance for his/her team to score points. If 1A wins the jumble, go to student 2A and give him/her a definition. He/she must give you the correct spelling of the vocabulary word which fits that definition. If he/she does, Team A scores a point, and you give student 3A a definition for which you expect a correctly spelled matching vocabulary word. Continue giving Team A definitions until some team member makes an incorrect response. An incorrect response sends the game back to the jumbled-word face off, this time with students 2A and 2B. Instead of repeating giving definitions to the first few students of each team, continue with the student after the one who gave the last incorrect response on the team. For example, if Team B wins the jumbled-word face-off, and student 5B gave the last incorrect answer for Team B, you would start this round of definition questions with student 6B, and so on. The team with the most points wins!

7. Have students write a story in which they correctly use as many vocabulary words as possible. Have students read their compositions orally! Post the most original compositions on your bulletin board!

8. Play I Have, Who Has? *NOTE this requires preparation in advance. On 3 x 5 cards, write a vocabulary word on one side and a definition to another word on the other side of the card. After you have completed a set, distribute the cards in a random order, keeping one for yourself. You will start the game by saying, "Who has [read the definition on your card]?" The student who has the word on his/her card that matches the definition shouts, "I Have [the word that matches your definition]!" He/she then turns his/her card over and says, "Who has [the definition on his/her card]?" and play continues until all the cards have been used.

9. Divide the class into two teams and play Baseball. The "pitcher" reads the definition of a word and in order to get a "hit," the "batter" must give the correct word to match the definition. For this game, though, only one strike is allowed! If the "batter" gives the correct word, he/she moves to first base and the next "batter" comes up for another word. Score is kept like baseball with three outs and the teams switching roles.

LESSON NINE

Objectives
1. To demonstrate analytical skills when reading poetry
2. To relate poetic works to Hermann Hesse's *Siddhartha*
3. To develop critical thinking skills through analyzing poetry
4. To practice cooperative learning skills by working in groups
5. To practice writing to inform
6. To evaluate students' writing skills

Activity 1
Break students into 3 groups and give each one of the following poems (on the pages that follow):
   An excerpt from "A Dialogue of Self and Soul" by William Butler Yeats
   An excerpt from "Song of Myself" by Walt Whitman
   "Beau Fleuve" by Susan Woodward

After students have read the poems, ask them to search for at least three poetic devices used by the poet (symbolism, imagery, personification, metaphor, simile, etc.) and how these devices were effective in creating meaning in the poem. What seems to be the message or theme of the poem? How might the theme of this poem relate to Siddhartha? Students must also answer the accompanying questions for the poem.

Activity 2
Provide enough copies so each student has a copy of all three poems. Each group will share its interpretation of the poem as well as its connection to *Siddhartha*.

Activity 3
Distribute Writing Assignment #2 and discuss the directions in detail. Each student will write an essay comparing ideas presented in the poem (one of the three) to a given section of Hermann Hesse's *Siddhartha*.

An Excerpt From **"A Dialogue of Self and Soul"**
by William Butler Yeats

My Soul: I summon to the winding ancient stair;
Set all your mind upon the steep ascent,
Upon the broken, crumbling battlement,
Upon the breathless starlit air,
'Upon the star that marks the hidden pole;
Fix every wandering thought upon
That quarter where all thought is done:
Who can distinguish darkness from the soul

...

My Self: A living man is blind and drinks his drop.
What matter if the ditches are impure?
What matter if I live it all once more?
Endure that toil of growing up;
The ignominy of boyhood; the distress
Of boyhood changing into man;
The unfinished man and his pain
Brought face to face with his own clumsiness;
The finished man among his enemies? --
How in the name of Heaven can he escape
That defiling and disfigured shape
The mirror of malicious eyes
Casts upon his eyes until at last
He thinks that shape must be his shape?
And what's the good of an escape
If honour find him in the wintry blast?
I am content to live it all again
And yet again, if it be life to pitch
Into the frog-spawn of a blind man's ditch,
A blind man battering blind men;
Or into that most fecund ditch of all,
The folly that man does
Or must suffer, if he woos
A proud woman not kindred of his soul.
I am content to follow to its source
Every event in action or in thought;
Measure the lot; forgive myself the lot!
When such as I cast out remorse
So great a sweetness flows into the breast
We must laugh and we must sing,
We are blest by everything,
Everything we look upon is blest.

Questions for "A Dialogue of Self and Soul" by William Butler Yeats

1. Fully describe the image as painted by the Soul. What might the "winding ancient stair" symbolize? How is the symbolism carried throughout the stanza?

2. Describe three images as portrayed by the Self. How are these images significant in helping the reader understand Yeats's meaning? What message is Yeats attempting to send to the reader through these images?

3. Why is Yeats "content to follow to its source/ Every event in action or in thought"? What does he mean by this? How does this idea relate to *Siddhartha*?

From "Song of Myself" (#51 and #52)
by Walt Whitman

The past and present wilt - I have fill'd them, emptied them.
And proceed to fill my next fold of the future.

Listener up there! what have you to confide to me?
Look in my face while I snuff the sidle of evening,
(Talk honestly, no one else hears you, and I stay only a minute longer.)

Do I contradict myself?
Very well then I contradict myself,
(I am large, I contain multitudes.)

I concentrate toward them that are nigh, I wait on the door-slab.

Who has done his day's work? who will soonest be through with his supper?
Who wishes to walk with me?

Will you speak before I am gone? will you prove already too late?

The spotted hawk swoops by and accuses me, he complains of my gab and my loitering.

I too am not a bit tamed, I too am untranslatable,
I sound my barbaric yawp over the roofs of the world.

The last scud of day holds back for me,
It flings my likeness after the rest and true as any on the shadow'd wilds,
It coaxes me to the vapor and the dusk.

I depart as air, I shake my white locks at the runaway sun,
I effuse my flesh in eddies, and drift it in lacy jags.

I bequeath myself to the dirt to grow from the grass I love,
If you want me again look for me under your boot-soles.

You will hardly know who I am or what I mean,
But I shall be good health to you nevertheless,
And filter and fibre your blood.

Failing to fetch me at first keep encouraged,
Missing me one place search another,
I stop somewhere waiting for you.

Questions for "Song of Myself" by Walt Whitman

1. What does Whitman mean when he says that he "is large" and "contains multitudes"? What imagery does Whitman use throughout the portion of the poem that may relate to this line?

2. What might be Whitman's "barbaric yawp" that he "sounds over the roofs of the world"? What does this line mean for the reader? What message is Whitman sending through this line?

3. Whitman says that if we want to find him again to "look for [him] under [our] boot-soles." What does this mean? How might this idea relate to messages in *Siddhartha*?

"Beau Fleuve"
by Susan R. Woodward

Drip, drip,
Drip, drip;
An icicle tip
Feeds a tiny spring below.
Drip, drip,
Drip, drip;
Carried away
By the water's gentle flow,
Effortlessly gliding
Around objects to and fro;
A rock here,
A stump there,
Form a meandering path
Winding its way
In search of a sister--
Separate tributaries fallen from the same tree;
Mere capillaries in the stream of life.
Two finally meet
And then another
And another.
With strength in numbers they carry forth
Babbling together as they travel.
Having no need for detours,
Rocks and stumps are hurdled over;
Each triumph is greeted with gurgles and splashes of laughter.
Love is nurtured and they flow like veins toward a common goal.
Further along, other families fall in.
Members mingle in a roar of introductions as everyone tries to talk at once;
Not until all are on even ground does the din dim.
Still more join in the journey from far-away places and their numbers swelled--
One river born from many streams,
Rolled in one blaze of blinding light.
Awed into silence, a higher power calls each to unite and follow;
None can ignore the call of the Current.
The love pulsating surges through every one;
They pick up the beat and flow forward drawing strength from one another
Until each comes to his destined course and is sent outward on his mission.
The river branches and reaches toward the surrounding land
Like oxygen-fed arteries carrying rich nourishment.
Life is sustained along the path as
Creatures of the forest
And photosynthesized friends are fed.

The outreach continues
With splintered streams
That eventually whittle down to
Trickling trails of life
Seeping into the ground.
Mettle is tested below the surface
With blind floundering
Hoping to be led toward Spring.
At last! Spring is found
And again emerges from the depths
To greet the newcomers from above;
Drip, drip,
Drip, drip,
Drip, drip.

Questions for "Beau Fleuve" by Susan R. Woodward

1. Explain the symbolism of the water cycle is it is described in the poem. What are the various stages of the water cycle that are described? What might be the significance of each stage?

2. What other cycle of life may be discovered throughout the poem? Why might Woodward have decided to weave the two together? How are they woven?

3. Examine the line length throughout the poem. How do the lines reflect what is being described in them? How might the symbolism of the Beau Fleuve (Beautiful River) be related to *Siddhartha*?

WRITING ASSIGNMENT #2 *Siddhartha*

PROMPT
You have read and studied three poems in class: "A Dialogue of Self and Soul" by William Butler Yeats, an excerpt from "Song of Myself" by Walt Whitman, and "Beau Fleuve" by Susan Woodward. Your assignment is to choose one of the poems and explain how it relates to Hermann Hesse's *Siddhartha*.

PREWRITING
Using your notes from the class discussions of the poem, identify the poet's use of at least three specific poetic techniques (imagery, symbolism, metaphor, etc.). How does the author's use of language enhance the message that the poet is trying to send? Locate the accompanying passage from *Siddhartha* that relates to your selected poem and connect the meaning of the poem to the ideas from the book. What message or theme do they have in common?

"A Dialogue of Self and Soul" to an excerpt from Chapter 12 (from "Listen, my friend!" through "These, Govinda, are some of the thoughts that are in my mind.")

"Song of Myself" to an excerpt from Chapter 12 (from "Siddhartha bent down, lifted a stone from the ground and held it in his hand" through "Govinda had listened in silence.")

"Beau Fleuve" to an excerpt from Chapter 11 (from "Siddhartha tried to listen better" through "Om--perfection.")

DRAFTING
Organizing your notes, write an essay that uses ideas from both works (the poem and the novel) that support a common message or theme. Show how the writer effectively uses literary/poetic techniques to help get the message across. Use a variety of sentence structures (simple, compound, complex, compound-complex) and incorporate at least five vocabulary words from the unit into your essay.

PROMPT
When you finish the rough draft of your paper, ask a student who sits near you to read it. After reading your rough draft, he/she should tell you what he/she liked best about your work, which parts were difficult to understand, and ways in which your work could be improved. Reread your paper considering your critic's comments and make the corrections you think are necessary.

PROOFREADING
Do a final proofreading of your paper double-checking your grammar, spelling, organization, and the clarity of your ideas.

LESSON TEN

<u>Objectives</u>
1. To demonstrate cooperative learning skills through working in pairs
2. To demonstrate comprehension of the use of figurative language
3. To develop critical thinking skills through the analysis of figurative language in *Siddhartha*

<u>Activity 1</u>
Write the following figurative language terms on the board:

Epithet
Metaphor
Simile
Imagery
Symbolism
Personification

Ask students what they think each term means. Give the dictionary definition and then create a working definition using the students' input. Write a definition next to each word on the board. Ask for possible examples from literature, movies, or television for each item and list them near the definitions.

<u>Activity 2</u>
Distribute the figurative language worksheets (found in the pages that follow) and tell students to work with a partner in analyzing Hesse's use of each of the literary devices in the examples given.

<u>Activity 3</u>
When students finish with the Figurative Language Worksheets, they may work on their essays for the poetry analysis or on their narrative poems.

<u>Activity 4</u>
This can be for homework.

Choose the questions from the Extra Discussion Questions/Writing Assignments which seem most appropriate for your students. A class discussion of these questions is most effective if students have been given the opportunity to formulate answers to the questions prior to the discussion. To this end, you may either have all the students formulate answers to all the questions, divide your class into groups and assign one or more questions to each group, or you could assign one question to each student in your class. The option you choose will make a difference in the amount of class time needed for this activity. The class discussion of these questions is scheduled for Lesson Thirteen.

Note: The use of graphic organizers may be helpful to students in preparing their answers. Encourage them to use any diagrams or graphics they feel are necessary or appropriate.

FIGURATIVE LANGUAGE WORKSHEET

Define the following examples of figurative language. Find the examples of the following examples of figurative language in the given chapters of Hermann Hesse's novel *Siddhartha*. Explain how the use of the figurative language is effective in getting Hesse's meaning across to his reader.

1. Epithet: _____

   Ch. 3: "Illustrious One" and "Perfect One"

   Ch. 12 "Venerable One" and "Worthy One"

2. Metaphor: _____

   Ch. 1: seeds of discontent

   Ch 4: snake (carried throughout the chapter)

   Ch. 5: throwing the stone in water

3. Simile: _____

   Ch. 2: a. hunter

         b. country ravaged with plague

   Ch. 6: a player who plays with a ball

   Ch. 7: the potter's wheel

4. Imagery: _____

    Ch. 2: description of physical changes that take place in Siddhartha

    Ch. 9: the river

    Ch. 10: Siddhartha's wound

5. Symbolism: _____

    Ch. 2: heron and jackal

    Ch. 5: Siddhartha's dream

    Ch 8: the spiral path

6. Personification: _____

    Ch. 7: the world

    Ch. 11: the river

EXTRA DISCUSSION QUESTIONS/WRITING ASSIGNMENTS *Siddhartha*

Interpretive

1. Discuss three positive and three negative character traits for Siddhartha. What do these traits show you about the kind of person Siddhartha is?
2. Discuss at least three specific character traits for each of the following characters: Govinda, the Ferryman, the Buddha, Siddhartha's son, Kamala, and Kamaswami. State the trait and give one example of it for each--3 traits with examples for each character.
3. What is the main conflict in Hermann Hesse's *Siddhartha*? Fully describe the conflict and how it is (or is not) resolved.
4. How does the fact that the novel is set in India play an important part in the events of the plot? What elements of life in India seem to play a key role in the main conflict? How does the setting differ from your own culture?
5. Examine each of Siddhartha's trials throughout his journey. What lesson does he learn from each?
6. Describe the climax of the novel. Where is Siddhartha's Apotheosis? What is the Ultimate Boon that he receives after his Road of Trials has been completed?

Critical

7. Explain what caused Siddhartha to leave home in Chapter One (his Call to Adventure). What tactics does he use to convince his father? What do these tactics show about his character? His father's character?
8. Describe the completed Departure Stage for Siddhartha. At what point does he cross the First Threshold? What does this mean for the young Siddhartha? What compels Siddhartha to continue on his journey?
9. Describe the Four Noble Truths of Buddhism. How are they reflected throughout the novel? What is the Eightfold Noble Path? How well does Siddhartha follow this path?
10. Explain the role Kamala plays in Siddhartha's learning. What does she represent on his Road of Trials? What about Kamaswami's role? Vasudeva's? Govinda's?
11. Explain the extended metaphor of the snake shedding its skin in Chapter 4. How does this mirror Siddhartha's experience?
12. What might be the motivation behind Siddhartha's discontent in the various places he travels and his eventual departure? What does he hope to learn?
13. Explain the symbolism of the river. What does it mean to the Ferryman? What does it come to mean to Siddhartha?
14. How does Siddhartha's seeing his father's face in his reflection in the river act as a source of irony? How does Siddhartha's son play a role in the irony?
15. Describe Siddhartha's "wound." What is its cause? How is the wound finally healed?
16. Siddhartha is reunited with Govinda at the end of the novel. How is it appropriate that this should be so according to Joseph Campbell's Hero's Journey? Explain Siddhartha's Return Stage.
17. Explain the main theme of this novel. What is Hermann Hesse's message to his readers?

Critical/Personal Response

18. Why do you suppose that Siddhartha sinks to the depth of despair and wishes for death? What led him to that point? What changes his mind?

19. Compare Siddhartha's treatment of his father with Siddhartha's son's treatment of Siddhartha. How might the story have been different if Siddhartha had found his son after he ran away?

20. Suppose Siddhartha had learned of Kamala's pregnancy before leaving and had decided to stay with her. How might the story have been different?

21. Suppose Siddhartha's son had accepted his father's ways and had stayed with him. What aspects of the plot and theme would have changed?

Personal Response

22. Did you enjoy reading this novel? Explain in detail using examples from the text supporting your view.

23. What age do you think is most appropriate for reading novels like *Siddhartha*? Why might age make a difference with this type of novel?

24. With which of the characters do you identify the most? Why?

LESSONS ELEVEN AND TWELVE

Objectives
1. To practice poetry writing skills by planning and writing a narrative poem
2. To practice cooperative skills by sharing ideas with a partner about the creation of a poem

Activity 1
Give students time to organize their journal entries and select information from their entries that they will use in creating their narrative poems. Create an atmosphere conducive to the creative process.

Activity 2
After students have selected the information from their journal entries that they wish to use in their poems, allow students to pair up and brainstorm how the ideas might be organized in poetic form and what types of figurative language might be incorporated into each poem. Let them brainstorm for about fifteen minutes for each partner, and then they may take their ideas and begin composing.

LESSON THIRTEEN

Objectives
1. To demonstrate an understanding of the novel beyond the factual questions asked in the study guide
2. To practice public speaking skills through sharing answers to discussion questions

Activity

Students will share their responses to the Extra Discussion Questions assigned during Lesson Ten. All students should take notes during the discussion. If your students are poor note-takers and need help, write important ideas on the board for students to copy.

LESSON FOURTEEN

<u>Objectives</u>
1. To demonstrate writing skills through the completion of an in-class writing assignment
2. To demonstrate the ability to work independently
3. To practice writing to persuade
4. To evaluate students' writing skills

<u>Activity</u>
Distribute Writing Assignment #3 and discuss the directions in detail. Give students the remaining class time to complete the assignment.

Students who finish this assignment early may work on other writing assignments or review their notes and study guides in preparation for the unit test.

WRITING ASSIGNMENT #3 *Siddhartha*

PROMPT
You have completed reading the novel *Siddhartha* in which a learned man allows his son to find his own way in the world after the young boy runs away from home. You must determine whether you agree or disagree with Siddhartha's treatment of his son. Was he right not to go find his son? Or did he do best by the young man in allowing him to make his own mistakes? Did Siddhartha follow through on his parental responsibilities, or did he neglect his duties? Choose only one position; do not try to argue both sides.

PREWRITING
Decide whether or not you agree with Siddhartha's actions and choose specific textual evidence from the novel that best supports your position.

DRAFTING
In your introduction, explain what it means to be an effective parent. At the end of your introduction, create a thesis statement in which you refer to Hermann Hesse's novel as support for your position on Siddhartha's treatment of his son.

Your body paragraphs should contain at least two specific reasons for your choice (complete with embedded quotations and parenthetical citations) that support your position.

Conclude your essay with some sort of a challenge to your reader with reference to parenting. Be sure to effectively incorporate at least five vocabulary words into your essay.

PROMPT
When you finish the rough draft of your paper, set it aside to bring to the next class meeting for a peer edit. After reading your rough draft, your editor will tell you what he/she liked best about your work, which parts were difficult to understand, and ways in which your work could be improved. Reread your paper considering your critic's comments, respond to the comments on the editing sheet, and make the corrections you think are necessary.

PROOFREADING
Do a final proofreading of your paper double-checking your grammar, spelling, organization, and the clarity of your ideas.

LESSON FIFTEEN

Objectives
1. To perform a critical analysis of essays
2. To accept constructive criticism, evaluate it, and determine a proper course of action with regard to written work
3. To complete Writing Assignment #3

Activity

Put students in pairs for peer editing and give each student a Peer Evaluation Form. Students will exchange their persuasive essays (Writing Assignment #3) and make comments regarding content, language use, and conventions as "Editors" of each others' work. Student editors will return the essays to the writers and then in the "Writer" portion of the form, the writers will respond to their peers editors' comments. After considering the editors' comments and responding to them, students will revise their essays as necessary.

After students have edited and revised their writing and turned in the essays to be graded, they may work on finishing their narrative poems if time remains in the class.

A Writing Evaluation Form is included for your convenience in case you would like to use it during or after grading student essays, perhaps as a basis for individual writing conferences with students.

Editor's Name _____ Date _____

Writer's Name _____ Assignment _____

Peer Editing for Writing Assignments

A. Was the writer's position clearly stated?
If your answer is "yes," be sure to tell the writer what he/she did that you especially liked. If your answer is "no," tell the writer what he/she could have included in order to write a better essay.

Editor: _____
_____
_____

Writer: _____
_____
_____

B. Did he/she provide enough details to support his/her position?
If your answer is "yes," be sure to tell the writer what you especially liked about his/her response. If your answer is "no," you must tell the writer how he/she could improve his/her response (adding specific details that were missed, connecting to position better, or adding embedded quotations).

Editor: _____
_____
_____

Writer: _____
_____
_____

C. Identify sentence type
Be sure to know the difference between simple, simple with compound subject, simple with compound predicate, compound, complex, and compound-complex. Using the first body paragraph, correctly identify each sentence type. If there is sufficient sentence structure variety, tell the writer what he/she did well. If not, explain what he/she could have done differently.

Sentence 1: _____ *Sentence 5:* _____

Sentence 2: _____ *Sentence 6:* _____

Sentence 3: _____ *Sentence 7:* _____

Sentence 4: _____ *Sentence 8:* _____

*Editor:*_____
_____
_____

*Writer:*_____
_____
_____

D. Address the Focus Correction Areas
   Did the writer follow the specifics of the essay such as (address each individually):

Organization:

Editor: _____

Writer: _____

Use of Vocabulary as Directed:

Editor: _____

Writer: _____

Citations from novel as support:

Editor: _____

Writer: _____

E. Check for Errors in Punctuation, Grammar, Spelling, etc.

Editor: _____

Writer: _____
Comments:

WRITING EVALUATION FORM - *Siddhartha*

Name _____ Date_____ Grade _____

Circle One For Each Item:

Grammar:	correct	errors noted on paper
Spelling:	correct	errors noted on paper
Punctuation:	correct	errors noted on paper
Legibility:	excellent	good fair poor
_____	excellent	good fair poor
_____	excellent	good fair poor

Strengths:

Weaknesses:

Comments/Suggestions:

LESSON SIXTEEN

Objectives
1. To review materials covered in the *Siddhartha* unit
2. To assess student readiness for testing

Activity

Choose one (or more) of the review activities below and use your class time accordingly.

UNIT REVIEW ACTIVITIES

1. Ask the class to make up a unit test for *Siddhartha*. The test should have 4 sections: matching, true/false, short answer, and essay. Students may use 1/2 period to make the test and then swap papers and use the other 1/2 class period to take a test a classmate has devised. (open book) You may want to use the unit test included in this packet or take questions from the students' unit tests to formulate your own test.

2. Take 1/2 period for students to make up true and false questions (including the answers). Collect the papers and divide the class into two teams. Draw a big tic-tac-toe board on the chalk board. Make one team X and one team O. Ask questions to each side, giving each student one turn. If the question is answered correctly, that student's team's letter (X or O) is placed in the box. If the answer is incorrect, no letter is placed in the box. The object is to get three in a row like tic-tac-toe. You may want to keep track of the number of games won for each team.

3. Take 1/2 period for students to make up questions (true/false and short answer). Collect the questions. Divide the class into two teams. You'll alternate asking questions to individual members of teams A & B (like in a spelling bee). The question keeps going from A to B until it is correctly answered, then a new question is asked. A correct answer does not allow the team to get another question. Correct answers are +2 points; incorrect answers are -1 point.

4. Have students pair up and quiz each other from their study guides and class notes.

5. Give students a *Siddhartha* crossword puzzle to complete.

6. Divide your class into two teams. Use *Siddhartha* crossword words with their letters jumbled as a word list. Student 1 from Team A faces off against Student 1 from Team B. You write the first jumbled word on the board. The first student (1A or 1B) to unscramble the word wins the chance for his/her team to score points. If 1A wins the jumble, go to student 2A and give him/her a clue. He/she must give you the correct word which matches that clue. If he/she does, Team A scores a point, and you give student 3A a clue for which you expect another correct response. Continue giving Team A clues until some team member makes an incorrect response. An incorrect response sends the game back to the jumbled-word face off, this time with students 2A and 2B. Instead of repeating giving clues to the first few students of each team, continue with the student after the one who gave the last incorrect response on the team. For example, if Team B wins the jumbled-word face-off, and student 5B gave the last incorrect answer for Team B, you would start this round of clue questions with student 6B, and so on. The team with the most points wins!

6. Play What's My Line?. This is similar to the old television show. Students assume the roles of different characters from the novel. One student gives clues to the class, or to a panel of contestants. The contestants try to guess the identity of the guest. Students may enjoy assisting you in creating rules and procedures for the game.

7. Play Jeopardy. Divide the class into two groups. Assign each group a category or book from the novel and have them devise answers for that category. Play the game according to the television show procedures.

8. Play Drawing in the Details. This is similar to Pictionary. Divide students into teams. A student from one team draws a scene from the novel. (You may want to specify the section.) Drawings should be kept simple, to keep the pace lively. Students in the opposing team locate the scene in their books and read it aloud. If they are incorrect, the illustrator's team has a chance to guess. Involve students in setting up a scoring system and any other necessary rules.

9. Play I Have, Who Has? *NOTE This requires preparation in advance. On 3x5 cards, write a clue word on one side and a clue/definition/question to another clue word on the other side of the card. Once you have completed a set, pass that cards out randomly, keeping one for yourself. You will start the game by saying, "Who Has..." and reading the definition/question on the card. The student who has the answer on his/her card that matches the definition/question shouts, "I Have..." and reads the answer. He/She then turns over the card and says "Who Has..." and play continues until the all the cards have been gone through.

10. Divide the class into two teams and play Baseball. The "pitcher" reads a question about the novel and in order to get a "hit" the "batter" must correctly answer the questions. For this game, though, only one strike is allowed! If the "batter" gives the correct answer, he/she moves to first base and the next "batter" comes up for another question. Score is kept like baseball with three outs and the teams switch places.

LESSON SEVENTEEN

Objectives
To assess students' understanding of the main events, ideas, and themes presented in *Siddhartha*

Activity
Distribute the unit tests, give students ample time to complete them, and collect the tests when students finish. Remember to collect assigned books prior to the end of the class period.

NOTES ABOUT THE UNIT TESTS IN THIS UNIT:

There are 5 different unit tests included in the LitPlan Teacher Pack. Two are short answer, two are multiple choice. There is one advanced short answer test. The answers to the advanced short answer test will be based on the discussions you have had during class and should be graded accordingly. You should choose the tests and/or test parts which best suit your needs. Matching and short answer tests have answer keys. For essay type questions, grade according to your own criteria based on class discussions and the level of your students. Also, you will need to choose vocabulary words to read orally for the vocabulary section of the short answer tests.

LESSON EIGHTEEN (Optional)

Objectives
1. To practice public speaking skills by reading poetry orally
2. To demonstrate the use of poetic techniques through sharing an original narrative poem

Activity

Give students time to present their narrative poems to the class. After each is read, have a short discussion about the poetic techniques used and, if appropriate, a short discussion about the student's personal Heroic Journey.

UNIT TESTS

Siddhartha SHORT ANSWER UNIT TEST 1

I. Matching

____ 1. SIDDHARTHA   A. Siddhartha became obsessed with this game.
____ 2. GOVINDA   B. Siddhartha and Govinda joined them.
____ 3. GOTAMA   C. Where the Ferryman goes to die
____ 4. KAMALA   D. It symbolizes the flow of life.
____ 5. KAMASWAMI   E. Faithful friend of Siddhartha since childhood
____ 6. SAMANAS   F. Son of a Brahmin who left home to find enlightenment
____ 7. RIVER   G. He is recognized by his complete peacefulness.
____ 8. WOODS   H. Siddhartha longs for it after leaving Kamala.
____ 9. STONE   I. Siddhartha's father is one.
____ 10. LOVE   J. The Buddha forbade his followers to bind themselves to this.
____ 11. DICE   K. One of the two animals Siddhartha associated himself with
____ 12. DEATH   L. Siddhartha tells Govinda that it could one day become a man.
____ 13. EXPERIENCE   M. He steals a boat and runs away.
____ 14. JETAVANA   N. Siddhartha desires to lose this.
____ 15. SON   O. Businessman who befriended Siddhartha
____ 16. SELF   P. It symbolizes the transformation of Siddhartha.
____ 17. SNAKE   Q. The Buddha
____ 18. BRAHMIN   R. The Buddha was given this place in which to live.
____ 19. HERON   S. Siddhartha believes he must gain this for himself.
____ 20. BUDDHA   T. Courtesan who loved Siddhartha

II. Short Answer

1. What is Siddhartha's "one single goal" on his first journey?

2. How does Siddhartha prove that he has mastered all that the Samana could teach him?

3. What does Siddhartha realize has left him "like the old skin that a snake sheds"?

4. What realization gives Siddhartha the feeling of awakening from a long dream?

5. When Siddhartha decides to be "present" in the world, what does he begin to notice about it?

6. The ferryman tells Siddhartha that one can learn much from something. What?

7. When Siddhartha's soul goes to sleep, what becomes more awakened?

8. How does Siddhartha's son behave while living in the hut by the river?

9. When Siddhartha bends over the water of the river and sees his reflection, of whose face is he reminded?

10. What does Govinda see in Siddhartha's face?

III. Essay
   Discuss at least three specific character traits for each of the following characters: Govinda, the Ferryman, the Buddha, Siddhartha's son, Kamala, and Kamaswami. State the trait and give one example of it for each--3 traits with examples for each character.

IV. Vocabulary
   Write the vocabulary words you are given. After writing them down, go back and write in their definitions.

Word	Definition
1	
2	
3	
4	
5	
6	
7	
8	
9	
10	

Siddhartha SHORT ANSWER UNIT TEST 1 Answer Key

I. Matching

F	1.	SIDDHARTHA	A.	Siddhartha became obsessed with this game.
E	2.	GOVINDA	B.	Siddhartha and Govinda joined them.
Q	3.	GOTAMA	C.	Where the Ferryman goes to die
T	4.	KAMALA	D.	It symbolizes the flow of life.
O	5.	KAMASWAMI	E.	Faithful friend of Siddhartha since childhood
B	6.	SAMANAS	F.	Son of a Brahmin who left home to find enlightenment
D	7.	RIVER	G.	He is recognized by his complete peacefulness.
C	8.	WOODS	H.	Siddhartha longs for it after leaving Kamala.
L	9.	STONE	I.	Siddhartha's father is one.
J	10.	LOVE	J.	The Buddha forbade his followers to bind themselves to this.
A	11.	DICE	K.	One of the two animals Siddhartha associated himself with
H	12.	DEATH	L.	Siddhartha tells Govinda that it could one day become a man.
S	13.	EXPERIENCE	M.	He steals a boat and runs away.
R	14.	JETAVANA	N.	Siddhartha desires to lose this.
M	15.	SON	O.	Businessman who befriended Siddhartha
N	16.	SELF	P.	It symbolizes the transformation of Siddhartha.
P	17.	SNAKE	Q.	The Buddha
I	18.	BRAHMIN	R.	The Buddha was given this place in which to live.
K	19.	HERON	S.	Siddhartha believes he must gain this for himself.
G	20.	BUDDHA	T.	Courtesan who loved Siddhartha

II. Short Answer
1. What is Siddhartha's "one single goal" on his first journey?
   He wishes to let the Self die.
2. How does Siddhartha prove that he has mastered all that the Samana could teach him?
   Siddhartha hypnotizes the eldest Samana, proving that he has mastered all that the Samana could teach him.
3. What does Siddhartha realize has left him "like the old skin that a snake sheds"?
   He has lost the desire to have teachers and to listen to their teaching.
4. What realization gives Siddhartha the feeling of awakening from a long dream?
   He realizes he has been afraid of being himself, and so he has tried to lose himself in the teachings of others.
5. When Siddhartha decides to be "present" in the world, what does he begin to notice about it?
   He notices the beauty of nature that he had never paid attention to before.
6. The ferryman tells Siddhartha that one can learn much from something. What?
   The ferryman tells Siddhartha that one can learn much from a river.
7. When Siddhartha's soul goes to sleep, what becomes more awakened?
   His senses become heightened.
8. How does Siddhartha's son behave while living in the hut by the river?
   He is a spoiled rich boy who refuses to do any work, and he is disrespectful of others.
9. When Siddhartha bends over the water of the river and sees his reflection, of whose face is he reminded?
   He is reminded of his father's face when he sees his own reflection.
10. What does Govinda see in Siddhartha's face?
    When Govinda looks into Siddhartha's face, he sees many other faces--hundreds, thousands, which seemed to be there all at the same time, and yet were all Siddhartha.

IV. Vocabulary
   Write the vocabulary words and definitions you will use for this test.

Word	Definition
1	
2	
3	
4	
5	
6	
7	
8	
9	
10	

Select the vocabulary words for Short Answer Test 1

Siddhartha SHORT ANSWER UNIT TEST 2

I. Matching

____ 1. SIDDHARTHA   A. Siddhartha's father is one.
____ 2. GOVINDA   B. Siddhartha lost the desire to have these.
____ 3. GOTAMA   C. He taught Siddhartha about the river.
____ 4. KAMALA   D. It means being receptive without a goal.
____ 5. KAMASWAMI   E. It means having a goal.
____ 6. VASUDEVA   F. Faithful friend of Siddhartha since childhood
____ 7. SAMANAS   G. The Buddha was given this place in which to live.
____ 8. LOVE   H. Siddhartha dreamed that it died and he threw it away.
____ 9. JETAVANA   I. Businessman who befriended Siddhartha
____ 10. SELF   J. Son of a Brahmin who left home to find enlightenment
____ 11. SNAKE   K. The Buddha forbade his followers to bind themselves to this.
____ 12. BRAHMIN   L. He is recognized by his complete peacefulness.
____ 13. HERON   M. It symbolizes the transformation of Siddhartha.
____ 14. BUDDHA   N. The Buddha
____ 15. TEACHERS   O. One of the two animals Siddhartha associated himself with
____ 16. BIRD   P. Siddhartha's son's means of escape
____ 17. TIME   Q. Siddhartha desires to lose this.
____ 18. FINDING   R. Courtesan who loved Siddhartha
____ 19. SEEKING   S. The secret from the river: there is no such thing as ___
____ 20. BOAT   T. Siddhartha and Govinda joined them.

II. Short Answer

1. What changes take place in Siddhartha while on the road with the Samanas?

2. What is Siddhartha's "one single goal" on his first journey?

3. Why is Siddhartha not very curious about the teachings of the Buddha?

4. What separates Govinda and Siddhartha?

5. What does Siddhartha dream as he slept in the ferryman's straw hut?

6. To what does Siddhartha compare those who have no "stillness and sanctuary to which [they] can retreat at any time"?

7. What becomes of Siddhartha's "glorious, exalted awakening" that he had experienced in his youth?

8. What are some of the things Siddhartha learns to do while living in the town after meeting Kamala and Kamaswami?

9. What things does Siddhartha claim he has had to experience "just in order to become a child again and begin anew"?

10. What is the first "secret from the river" that Siddhartha learns?

11. What does Vasudeva suggest Siddhartha should do for his son?

III. Essay

Examine each of Siddhartha's trials throughout his journey. What lesson does he learn from each?

IV. Vocabulary
   Write the vocabulary words you are given. After writing them down, go back and write in their definitions.

Word	Definition
1	
2	
3	
4	
5	
6	
7	
8	
9	
10	

Siddhartha SHORT ANSWER UNIT TEST 2 Answer Key

I. Matching

J	1.	SIDDHARTHA	A.	Siddhartha's father is one.
F	2.	GOVINDA	B.	Siddhartha lost the desire to have these.
N	3.	GOTAMA	C.	He taught Siddhartha about the river.
R	4.	KAMALA	D.	It means being receptive without a goal.
I	5.	KAMASWAMI	E.	It means having a goal.
C	6.	VASUDEVA	F.	Faithful friend of Siddhartha since childhood
T	7.	SAMANAS	G.	The Buddha was given this place in which to live.
K	8.	LOVE	H.	Siddhartha dreamed that it died and he threw it away.
G	9.	JETAVANA	I.	Businessman who befriended Siddhartha
Q	10.	SELF	J.	Son of a Brahmin who left home to find enlightenment
M	11.	SNAKE	K.	The Buddha forbade his followers to bind themselves to this.
A	12.	BRAHMIN	L.	He is recognized by his complete peacefulness.
O	13.	HERON	M.	It symbolizes the transformation of Siddhartha.
L	14.	BUDDHA	N.	The Buddha
B	15.	TEACHERS	O.	One of the two animals Siddhartha associated himself with
H	16.	BIRD	P.	Siddhartha's son's means of escape
S	17.	TIME	Q.	Siddhartha desires to lose this.
D	18.	FINDING	R.	Courtesan who loved Siddhartha
E	19.	SEEKING	S.	The secret from the river: there is no such thing as ___
P	20.	BOAT	T.	Siddhartha and Govinda joined them.

II. Short Answer

1. What changes take place in Siddhartha while on the road with the Samanas?
   He becomes thin from fasting, his nails grow long, he gives away his clothes, he snarls at women, and he looks at well-dressed people with contempt.

2. What is Siddhartha's "one single goal" on his first journey?
   He wishes to let the Self die.

3. Why is Siddhartha not very curious about the teachings of the Buddha?
   He does not think the Buddha can teach him anything new.

4. What separates Govinda and Siddhartha?
   Govinda joins the Buddha's community, and Siddhartha moves on.

5. What does Siddhartha dream as he slept in the ferryman's straw hut?
   Siddhartha dreams that Govinda stands before him asking, "Why did you leave me?" Govinda then turns into a woman from whose breast Siddhartha drinks and becomes intoxicated with pleasure.

6. To what does Siddhartha compare those who have no "stillness and sanctuary to which [they] can retreat at any time"?
   Siddhartha compares them to falling leaves that drift and turn in the air but have no direction.

7. What becomes of Siddhartha's "glorious, exalted awakening" that he had experienced in his youth?
   It becomes a memory and passes away.

8. What are some of the things Siddhartha learns to do while living in the town after meeting Kamala and Kamaswami?
   He learns to transact business, exercise power over people, amuse himself with women, wear fine clothes, command servants, bathe in sweet-smelling waters, eat rich foods, and drink wine.

9. What things does Siddhartha claim he has had to experience "just in order to become a child again and begin anew"?
   He has had to experience stupidity, vices, error, nausea, disillusionment, and sorrow.

10. What is the first "secret from the river" that Siddhartha learns?
    He learns that there is no such thing as time. "The river is everywhere at the same time, at the source and at the mouth, at the waterfall, at the ferry, at the current, in the ocean, and in the mountains, everywhere, and that the present only exists for it."

11. What does Vasudeva suggest Siddhartha should do for his son?
    Vasudeva suggests that Siddhartha should take the boy back to the town where he grew up and find him a life that includes people his own age.

IV. Vocabulary
   Write the vocabulary words and definitions you will use for this test.

Word	Definition
1	
2	
3	
4	
5	
6	
7	
8	
9	
10	

Select the vocabulary words for Short Answer Test 2

Siddhartha ADVANCED SHORT ANSWER UNIT TEST

I. Matching

____	1.	SIDDHARTHA	A.	The Buddha was given this place in which to live.
____	2.	GOVINDA	B.	Siddhartha longs for it after leaving Kamala.
____	3.	GOTAMA	C.	Siddhartha's father is one.
____	4.	KAMALA	D.	It means having a goal.
____	5.	KAMASWAMI	E.	The Buddha
____	6.	VASUDEVA	F.	He taught Siddhartha about the river.
____	7.	SAMANAS	G.	Faithful friend of Siddhartha since childhood
____	8.	RIVER	H.	Son of a Brahmin who left home to find enlightenment
____	9.	WOODS	I.	It means being receptive without a goal.
____	10.	STONE	J.	Siddhartha became obsessed with this game.
____	11.	LOVE	K.	It symbolizes the flow of life.
____	12.	DICE	L.	He is recognized by his complete peacefulness.
____	13.	DEATH	M.	Where the Ferryman goes to die
____	14.	JETAVANA	N.	Siddhartha lost the desire to have these.
____	15.	SNAKE	O.	It symbolizes the transformation of Siddhartha.
____	16.	BRAHMIN	P.	Siddhartha tells Govinda that it could one day become a man.
____	17.	BUDDHA	Q.	Courtesan who loved Siddhartha
____	18.	TEACHERS	R.	The Buddha forbade his followers to bind themselves to this.
____	19.	FINDING	S.	Siddhartha and Govinda joined them.
____	20.	SEEKING	T.	Businessman who befriended Siddhartha

II. Short Answer
1. Discuss three positive and three negative character traits for Siddhartha. What do these traits show you about the kind of person Siddhartha is?

2. What is the main conflict in Hermann Hesse's *Siddhartha*? Fully describe the conflict and how it is (or is not) resolved.

3. Describe the climax of the novel. Where is Siddhartha's Apotheosis? What is the Ultimate Boon that he receives after his Road of Trials has been completed?

4. Describe the completed Departure Stage for Siddhartha. At what point does he cross the First Threshold? What does this mean for the young Siddhartha? What compels Siddhartha to continue on his journey?

5. Explain the extended metaphor of the snake shedding its skin in Chapter 4. How does this mirror Siddhartha's experience?

6. How does Siddhartha's seeing his father's face in his reflection in the river act as a source of irony? How does Siddhartha's son play a role in the irony?

7. Describe Siddhartha's "wound." What is its cause? How is the wound finally healed?

8. Why do you suppose that Siddhartha sinks to the depth of despair and wishes for death? What led him to that point? What changes his mind?

III. Essay

Describe the Four Noble Truths of Buddhism. How are they reflected throughout the novel? What is the Eightfold Noble Path? How well does Siddhartha follow this path?

IV. Vocabulary
   A. Write the vocabulary words you are given. After writing them down, go back and write in their definitions.

Word	Definition
1	
2	
3	
4	
5	
6	
7	
8	
9	
10	

   B. Write a paragraph about the book using 8 of the 10 vocabulary words above.

Siddhartha ADVANCED SHORT ANSWER UNIT TEST Answer Key

I. Matching

H	1.	SIDDHARTHA	A.	The Buddha was given this place in which to live.
G	2.	GOVINDA	B.	Siddhartha longs for it after leaving Kamala.
E	3.	GOTAMA	C.	Siddhartha's father is one.
Q	4.	KAMALA	D.	It means having a goal.
T	5.	KAMASWAMI	E.	The Buddha
F	6.	VASUDEVA	F.	He taught Siddhartha about the river.
S	7.	SAMANAS	G.	Faithful friend of Siddhartha since childhood
K	8.	RIVER	H.	Son of a Brahmin who left home to find enlightenment
M	9.	WOODS	I.	It means being receptive without a goal.
P	10.	STONE	J.	Siddhartha became obsessed with this game.
R	11.	LOVE	K.	It symbolizes the flow of life.
J	12.	DICE	L.	He is recognized by his complete peacefulness.
B	13.	DEATH	M.	Where the Ferryman goes to die
A	14.	JETAVANA	N.	Siddhartha lost the desire to have these.
O	15.	SNAKE	O.	It symbolizes the transformation of Siddhartha.
C	16.	BRAHMIN	P.	Siddhartha tells Govinda that it could one day become a man.
L	17.	BUDDHA	Q.	Courtesan who loved Siddhartha
N	18.	TEACHERS	R.	The Buddha forbade his followers to bind themselves to this.
I	19.	FINDING	S.	Siddhartha and Govinda joined them.
D	20.	SEEKING	T.	Businessman who befriended Siddhartha

IV. Vocabulary
   Write the vocabulary words and definitions you will use for this test.

Word	Definition
1	
2	
3	
4	
5	
6	
7	
8	
9	
10	

Select the vocabulary words for the Advanced Short Answer Test

Siddhartha MULTIPLE CHOICE UNIT TEST 1

I. Matching

___ 1. SIDDHARTHA   A. Siddhartha believes he must gain this for himself.
___ 2. GOVINDA   B. One of the two animals Siddhartha associated himself with
___ 3. GOTAMA   C. Siddhartha and Govinda joined them.
___ 4. KAMALA   D. Faithful friend of Siddhartha since childhood
___ 5. KAMASWAMI   E. He is recognized by his complete peacefulness.
___ 6. VASUDEVA   F. The Buddha was given this place in which to live.
___ 7. SAMANAS   G. He taught Siddhartha about the river.
___ 8. RIVER   H. Siddhartha desires to lose this.
___ 9. STONE   I. The Buddha forbade his followers to bind themselves to this.
___ 10. LOVE   J. Businessman who befriended Siddhartha
___ 11. DEATH   K. Son of a Brahmin who left home to find enlightenment
___ 12. EXPERIENCE   L. It symbolizes the transformation of Siddhartha.
___ 13. JETAVANA   M. Siddhartha longs for it after leaving Kamala.
___ 14. SELF   N. The Buddha
___ 15. SNAKE   O. Courtesan who loved Siddhartha
___ 16. HERON   P. It means having a goal.
___ 17. BUDDHA   Q. Siddhartha dreamed that it died and he threw it away.
___ 18. BIRD   R. It symbolizes the flow of life.
___ 19. FINDING   S. It means being receptive without a goal.
___ 20. SEEKING   T. Siddhartha tells Govinda that it could one day become a man.

II. Multiple Choice

1. What has caused Siddhartha "to feel the seeds of discontent within him"?
   A. Siddhartha desires to travel to see far away lands.
   B. Siddhartha cannot find his one true love.
   C. Siddhartha wishes to attend a university.
   D. Siddhartha believes that he has obtained all the knowledge that his father and teachers can offer, but it is not enough.

2. When Siddhartha's soul goes to sleep, what becomes more awakened?
   A. His consciousness
   B. His intellect
   C. His senses
   D. His enlightenment

3. To what does Siddhartha compare those who have no "stillness and sanctuary to which [they] can retreat at any time"?
   A. He compares them to a snake shedding its skin.
   B. He compares them to falling leaves that have no direction.
   C. He compares them to the flowing river.
   D. He compares them to a heron flying high in the sky.

4. What does Siddhartha dream as he slept in the ferryman's straw hut?
   A. He dreams he floats along the river on a raft made of gold.
   B. He dreams Govinda becomes a woman and he drinks from her breast.
   C. He dreams his father dies.
   D. He dreams he drowns in the river.

5. When Siddhartha decides to be "present" in the world, what does he begin to notice about it?
   A. He notices the beauty of nature that he had never paid attention to before.
   B. He notices how large the world really is outside of his little village.
   C. He notices the ugliness of what man has done to nature.
   D. He notices how petty people act towards each other.

6. What separates Govinda and Siddhartha?
    A. Siddhartha returns to his home village.
    B. Siddhartha is bitten by a poisonous snake and dies.
    C. Govinda is discouraged and leaves the Samanas for a life of the senses.
    D. Govinda joins the Buddha's community.

7. Why is Siddhartha not very curious about the teachings of the Buddha?
    A. Siddhartha has not heard of the Buddha.
    B. Since the Buddha is not a Samana, Siddhartha does not care to listen to him.
    C. He does not think the Buddha can teach him anything new.
    D. He does not agree with what the Buddha teaches.

8. How does Siddhartha prove that he has mastered all that the Samana can teach him?
    A. Siddhartha hypnotizes the eldest Samana.
    B. Siddhartha reads the old man's mind.
    C. Siddhartha prays and makes it rain.
    D. Siddhartha fasts for seven days.

9. When Siddhartha first leaves home, where does he want to go to try to acquire more knowledge?
    A. He wants to travel with the ascetics and become a Samana.
    B. He wants to go to China.
    C. He wants to go to the University of Padua.
    D. He wants to follow the Buddha and learn all the Buddha has to teach.

10. What does Vasudeva suggest Siddhartha should do for his son?
    A. Siddhartha should send the boy to the Buddha's community.
    B. Siddhartha should severely punish the boy for his behavior.
    C. Siddhartha should send the boy off to school.
    D. Siddhartha should take the boy back to town to be with people his own age.

III. Essay

Explain the role Kamala plays in Siddhartha's learning. What does she represent on his Road of Trials? What about Kamaswami's role? Vasudeva's? Govinda's?

IV. Vocabulary

____ 1. CHASM   A. Respected
____ 2. PALLIATIVE   B. Characteristic of, proper to, or customary for slaves
____ 3. RENOUNCED   C. Thoughtful or sympathetic regard or respect
____ 4. IMPERTURBABLE   D. Boredom; dissatisfaction resulting from lack of interest
____ 5. MUTILATE   E. Downward slope
____ 6. GUILD   F. Can't be bothered, agitated, or upset
____ 7. ARDENT   G. Characterized by intense feeling
____ 8. INDOLENT   H. Miserable; very unfortunate
____ 9. SERVILE   I. Inactive; lethargic
____ 10. DECLIVITY   J. Something that makes pain or sorrow easier to bear
____ 11. WRETCHED   K. Belonging to a thing by its very nature
____ 12. ENNUI   L. Constant in effort; working diligently at a task
____ 13. TRANSITORY   M. Not lasting, permanent, or eternal
____ 14. ASSIDUOUS   N. Try hard
____ 15. STRIVE   O. Deep cleft in the ground; gorge
____ 16. DEVOUT   P. Injure or disfigure by removing or irreparably damaging parts
____ 17. CONSIDERATION   Q. Gave up or put aside voluntarily
____ 18. DISPEL   R. Cause to vanish; get rid of
____ 19. ESTEEMED   S. Pious; religious; devoted to divine worship or service
____ 20. INTRINSIC   T. Association of tradesmen

Siddhartha MULTIPLE CHOICE UNIT TEST 1 Answer Key

I. Matching

K	1.	SIDDHARTHA	A.	Siddhartha believes he must gain this for himself.
D	2.	GOVINDA	B.	One of the two animals Siddhartha associated himself with
N	3.	GOTAMA	C.	Siddhartha and Govinda joined them.
O	4.	KAMALA	D.	Faithful friend of Siddhartha since childhood
J	5.	KAMASWAMI	E.	He is recognized by his complete peacefulness.
G	6.	VASUDEVA	F.	The Buddha was given this place in which to live.
C	7.	SAMANAS	G.	He taught Siddhartha about the river.
R	8.	RIVER	H.	Siddhartha desires to lose this.
T	9.	STONE	I.	The Buddha forbade his followers to bind themselves to this.
I	10.	LOVE	J.	Businessman who befriended Siddhartha
M	11.	DEATH	K.	Son of a Brahmin who left home to find enlightenment
A	12.	EXPERIENCE	L.	It symbolizes the transformation of Siddhartha.
F	13.	JETAVANA	M.	Siddhartha longs for it after leaving Kamala.
H	14.	SELF	N.	The Buddha
L	15.	SNAKE	O.	Courtesan who loved Siddhartha
B	16.	HERON	P.	It means having a goal.
E	17.	BUDDHA	Q.	Siddhartha dreamed that it died and he threw it away.
Q	18.	BIRD	R.	It symbolizes the flow of life.
S	19.	FINDING	S.	It means being receptive without a goal.
P	20.	SEEKING	T.	Siddhartha tells Govinda that it could one day become a man.

II. Multiple Choice

D 1. What has caused Siddhartha "to feel the seeds of discontent within him"?
   A. Siddhartha desires to travel to see far away lands.
   B. Siddhartha cannot find his one true love.
   C. Siddhartha wishes to attend a university.
   D. Siddhartha believes that he has obtained all the knowledge that his father and teachers can offer, but it is not enough.

C 2. When Siddhartha's soul goes to sleep, what becomes more awakened?
   A. His consciousness
   B. His intellect
   C. His senses
   D. His enlightenment

B 3. To what does Siddhartha compare those who have no "stillness and sanctuary to which [they] can retreat at any time"?
   A. He compares them to a snake shedding its skin.
   B. He compares them to falling leaves that have no direction.
   C. He compares them to the flowing river.
   D. He compares them to a heron flying high in the sky.

B 4. What does Siddhartha dream as he slept in the ferryman's straw hut?
   A. He dreams he floats along the river on a raft made of gold.
   B. He dreams Govinda becomes a woman and he drinks from her breast.
   C. He dreams his father dies.
   D. He dreams he drowns in the river.

A 5. When Siddhartha decides to be "present" in the world, what does he begin to notice about it?
   A. He notices the beauty of nature that he had never paid attention to before.
   B. He notices how large the world really is outside of his little village.
   C. He notices the ugliness of what man has done to nature.
   D. He notices how petty people act towards each other.

D 6. What separates Govinda and Siddhartha?
   A. Siddhartha returns to his home village.
   B. Siddhartha is bitten by a poisonous snake and dies.
   C. Govinda is discouraged and leaves the Samanas for a life of the senses.
   D. Govinda joins the Buddha's community.

C 7. Why is Siddhartha not very curious about the teachings of the Buddha?
   A. Siddhartha has not heard of the Buddha.
   B. Since the Buddha is not a Samana, Siddhartha does not care to listen to him.
   C. He does not think the Buddha can teach him anything new.
   D. He does not agree with what the Buddha teaches.

A 8. How does Siddhartha prove that he has mastered all that the Samana can teach him?
   A. Siddhartha hypnotizes the eldest Samana.
   B. Siddhartha reads the old man's mind.
   C. Siddhartha prays and makes it rain.
   D. Siddhartha fasts for seven days.

A 9. When Siddhartha first leaves home, where does he want to go to try to acquire more knowledge?
   A. He wants to travel with the ascetics and become a Samana.
   B. He wants to go to China.
   C. He wants to go to the University of Padua.
   D. He wants to follow the Buddha and learn all the Buddha has to teach.

D 10. What does Vasudeva suggest Siddhartha should do for his son?
   A. Siddhartha should send the boy to the Buddha's community.
   B. Siddhartha should severely punish the boy for his behavior.
   C. Siddhartha should send the boy off to school.
   D. Siddhartha should take the boy back to town to be with people his own age.

IV. Vocabulary

O	1.	CHASM	A.	Respected
J	2.	PALLIATIVE	B.	Characteristic of, proper to, or customary for slaves
Q	3.	RENOUNCED	C.	Thoughtful or sympathetic regard or respect
F	4.	IMPERTURBABLE	D.	Boredom; dissatisfaction resulting from lack of interest
P	5.	MUTILATE	E.	Downward slope
T	6.	GUILD	F.	Can't be bothered, agitated, or upset
G	7.	ARDENT	G.	Characterized by intense feeling
I	8.	INDOLENT	H.	Miserable; very unfortunate
B	9.	SERVILE	I.	Inactive; lethargic
E	10.	DECLIVITY	J.	Something that makes pain or sorrow easier to bear
H	11.	WRETCHED	K.	Belonging to a thing by its very nature
D	12.	ENNUI	L.	Constant in effort; working diligently at a task
M	13.	TRANSITORY	M.	Not lasting, permanent, or eternal
L	14.	ASSIDUOUS	N.	Try hard
N	15.	STRIVE	O.	Deep cleft in the ground; gorge
S	16.	DEVOUT	P.	Injure or disfigure by removing or irreparably damaging parts
C	17.	CONSIDERATION	Q.	Gave up or put aside voluntarily
R	18.	DISPEL	R.	Cause to vanish; get rid of
A	19.	ESTEEMED	S.	Pious; religious; devoted to divine worship or service
K	20.	INTRINSIC	T.	Association of tradesmen

Siddhartha MULTIPLE CHOICE UNIT TEST 2

I. Matching

____ 1.	SIDDHARTHA	A.	Businessman who befriended Siddhartha
____ 2.	GOVINDA	B.	The Buddha forbade his followers to bind themselves to this.
____ 3.	GOTAMA	C.	Son of a Brahmin who left home to find enlightenment
____ 4.	KAMALA	D.	Siddhartha's father is one.
____ 5.	KAMASWAMI	E.	Siddhartha believes he must gain this for himself.
____ 6.	VASUDEVA	F.	Faithful friend of Siddhartha since childhood
____ 7.	SAMANAS	G.	Siddhartha tells Govinda that it could one day become a man.
____ 8.	RIVER	H.	Courtesan who loved Siddhartha
____ 9.	STONE	I.	The Buddha was given this place in which to live.
____ 10.	LOVE	J.	He taught Siddhartha about the river.
____ 11.	DEATH	K.	He steals a boat and runs away.
____ 12.	EXPERIENCE	L.	It symbolizes the flow of life.
____ 13.	JETAVANA	M.	Siddhartha dreamed that it died and he threw it away.
____ 14.	SON	N.	The Buddha
____ 15.	SNAKE	O.	It symbolizes the transformation of Siddhartha.
____ 16.	BRAHMIN	P.	He is recognized by his complete peacefulness.
____ 17.	HERON	Q.	Siddhartha longs for it after leaving Kamala.
____ 18.	BUDDHA	R.	The secret from the river: there is no such thing as ___
____ 19.	BIRD	S.	One of the two animals Siddhartha associated himself with
____ 20.	TIME	T.	Siddhartha and Govinda joined them.

II. Multiple Choice

1. What is Siddhartha's "one single goal" on his first journey?
   A. He wishes to find his one true love.
   B. He wishes to see the whole world.
   C. He wishes to let the Self die.
   D. He wishes to find enlightenment.

2. What does the Buddha warn Siddhartha to be on his guard against?
   A. Greed
   B. Loose women
   C. Too much cleverness
   D. False teachers

3. When Siddhartha decides to be "present" in the world, what does he begin to notice about it?
   A. He notices the ugliness of what man has done to nature.
   B. He notices the beauty of nature that he had never paid attention to before.
   C. He notices how large the world really is outside of his little village.
   D. He notices how petty people act towards each other.

4. What services does Siddhartha say he can perform for Kamaswami?
   A. He can learn to love.
   B. He can do accounting and bookkeeping.
   C. He can think, he can wait, and he can fast.
   D. He can guide the ferry across the river.

5. When Siddhartha's soul goes to sleep, what becomes more awakened?
   A. His consciousness
   B. His enlightenment
   C. His intellect
   D. His senses

6. Which is NOT one of the things Siddhartha claims he has had to experience in order to become a child again and begin anew?
   A. Love
   B. Disillusionment
   C. Stupidity
   D. Nausea

7. What becomes of Kamala?
   A. She becomes a member of the Buddha's community.
   B. She is bitten by a snake and dies.
   C. She reveals her love for Siddhartha, and he takes her as his wife.
   D. She drowns in the river.

8. What knowledge does Siddhartha possess that he many times "doubted...was of such great value?"
   A. He possesses the truth that life is a cyclical path that spirals outward.
   B. He possesses the hope of the river.
   C. He possesses the knowledge of what happened to his son.
   D. He possesses the consciousness of the unity of life.

9. To what realization does Siddhartha come after seeing his reflection in the water?
   A. He realizes that his father had suffered the same sorrows at Siddhartha's leaving that Siddhartha now suffers at the leaving of his own son.
   B. He realizes how he had cheated Kamaswami, and he feels remorse.
   C. He realizes that he has grown old and has wasted much of his life in sin.
   D. He realizes how much he truly loved Kamala.

10. What does Govinda see in Siddhartha's face?
    A. He sees his own reflection in Siddhartha's eyes.
    B. He sees the sense of peace that comes from attaining Nirvana.
    C. He sees the pain of the loss of Siddhartha's son and a life ill-spent in sin.
    D. He sees many other faces all at the same time, and yet they are all Siddhartha.

III. Composition
   Suppose Siddhartha's son had accepted his father's ways and had stayed with him. What aspects of the plot and theme would have changed?

IV. Vocabulary

___ 1.	AVARICIOUS	A.	Bold resistance to authority or any opposing force
___ 2.	ONEROUS	B.	Undeniably; unarguably
___ 3.	AUSTERE	C.	Hurting with a sharp, usually superficial, stinging pain
___ 4.	IRREFUTABLY	D.	One who came before another in holding an office or position
___ 5.	EQUANIMITY	E.	Quality of being calm and even-tempered; composure
___ 6.	DIVERSITIES	F.	Sacred or holy place; place of safety
___ 7.	ARTISAN	G.	Sunk below the surface
___ 8.	COURTESAN	H.	Immoderately desirous of wealth or gain; greedy
___ 9.	HASTINESS	I.	Things that are unimportant or frivolous
___ 10.	SANCTUARY	J.	With overly-eager speed and possible carelessness
___ 11.	SUBMERGED	K.	Points or aspects in which things differ
___ 12.	INERTIA	L.	Tendency to remain at rest or resist motion or change
___ 13.	INCIPIENT	M.	Act of atoning for sins or wrongdoing
___ 14.	EXPIATION	N.	Burdensome; oppressive; troublesome; causing hardship
___ 15.	DEFIANCE	O.	Person skilled in an applied art; craftsman
___ 16.	SMARTING	P.	Capable of being easily communicated or transmitted
___ 17.	TRIVIALITIES	Q.	Severe in manner or appearance; strict
___ 18.	DISCLOSE	R.	Prostitute or paramour, esp. one associating with noblemen
___ 19.	PREDECESSOR	S.	Beginning to exist or appear
___ 20.	COMMUNICABLE	T.	Make known; reveal; uncover

Siddhartha MULTIPLE CHOICE UNIT TEST 2 Answer Key

I. Matching

C	1.	SIDDHARTHA	A.	Businessman who befriended Siddhartha
F	2.	GOVINDA	B.	The Buddha forbade his followers to bind themselves to this.
N	3.	GOTAMA	C.	Son of a Brahmin who left home to find enlightenment
H	4.	KAMALA	D.	Siddhartha's father is one.
A	5.	KAMASWAMI	E.	Siddhartha believes he must gain this for himself.
J	6.	VASUDEVA	F.	Faithful friend of Siddhartha since childhood
T	7.	SAMANAS	G.	Siddhartha tells Govinda that it could one day become a man.
L	8.	RIVER	H.	Courtesan who loved Siddhartha
G	9.	STONE	I.	The Buddha was given this place in which to live.
B	10.	LOVE	J.	He taught Siddhartha about the river.
Q	11.	DEATH	K.	He steals a boat and runs away.
E	12.	EXPERIENCE	L.	It symbolizes the flow of life.
I	13.	JETAVANA	M.	Siddhartha dreamed that it died and he threw it away.
K	14.	SON	N.	The Buddha
O	15.	SNAKE	O.	It symbolizes the transformation of Siddhartha.
D	16.	BRAHMIN	P.	He is recognized by his complete peacefulness.
S	17.	HERON	Q.	Siddhartha longs for it after leaving Kamala.
P	18.	BUDDHA	R.	The secret from the river: there is no such thing as ___
M	19.	BIRD	S.	One of the two animals Siddhartha associated himself with
R	20.	TIME	T.	Siddhartha and Govinda joined them.

II. Multiple Choice

C 1. What is Siddhartha's "one single goal" on his first journey?
    A. He wishes to find his one true love.
    B. He wishes to see the whole world.
    C. He wishes to let the Self die.
    D. He wishes to find enlightenment.

C 2. What does the Buddha warn Siddhartha to be on his guard against?
    A. Greed
    B. Loose women
    C. Too much cleverness
    D. False teachers

B 3. When Siddhartha decides to be "present" in the world, what does he begin to notice about it?
    A. He notices the ugliness of what man has done to nature.
    B. He notices the beauty of nature that he had never paid attention to before.
    C. He notices how large the world really is outside of his little village.
    D. He notices how petty people act towards each other.

C 4. What services does Siddhartha say he can perform for Kamaswami?
    A. He can learn to love.
    B. He can do accounting and bookkeeping.
    C. He can think, he can wait, and he can fast.
    D. He can guide the ferry across the river.

D 5. When Siddhartha's soul goes to sleep, what becomes more awakened?
    A. His consciousness
    B. His enlightenment
    C. His intellect
    D. His senses

A 6. Which is NOT one of the things Siddhartha claims he has had to experience in order to become a child again and begin anew?
    A. Love
    B. Disillusionment
    C. Stupidity
    D. Nausea

B 7. What becomes of Kamala?
- A. She becomes a member of the Buddha's community.
- B. She is bitten by a snake and dies.
- C. She reveals her love for Siddhartha, and he takes her as his wife.
- D. She drowns in the river.

D 8. What knowledge does Siddhartha possess that he many times "doubted...was of such great value?"
- A. He possesses the truth that life is a cyclical path that spirals outward.
- B. He possesses the hope of the river.
- C. He possesses the knowledge of what happened to his son.
- D. He possesses the consciousness of the unity of life.

A 9. To what realization does Siddhartha come after seeing his reflection in the water?
- A. He realizes that his father had suffered the same sorrows at Siddhartha's leaving that Siddhartha now suffers at the leaving of his own son.
- B. He realizes how he had cheated Kamaswami, and he feels remorse.
- C. He realizes that he has grown old and has wasted much of his life in sin.
- D. He realizes how much he truly loved Kamala.

D 10. What does Govinda see in Siddhartha's face?
- A. He sees his own reflection in Siddhartha's eyes.
- B. He sees the sense of peace that comes from attaining Nirvana.
- C. He sees the pain of the loss of Siddhartha's son and a life ill-spent in sin.
- D. He sees many other faces all at the same time, and yet they are all Siddhartha.

IV. Vocabulary

H	1.	AVARICIOUS	A.	Bold resistance to authority or any opposing force
N	2.	ONEROUS	B.	Undeniably; unarguably
Q	3.	AUSTERE	C.	Hurting with a sharp, usually superficial, stinging pain
B	4.	IRREFUTABLY	D.	One who came before another in holding an office or position
E	5.	EQUANIMITY	E.	Quality of being calm and even-tempered; composure
K	6.	DIVERSITIES	F.	Sacred or holy place; place of safety
O	7.	ARTISAN	G.	Sunk below the surface
R	8.	COURTESAN	H.	Immoderately desirous of wealth or gain; greedy
J	9.	HASTINESS	I.	Things that are unimportant or frivolous
F	10.	SANCTUARY	J.	With overly-eager speed and possible carelessness
G	11.	SUBMERGED	K.	Points or aspects in which things differ
L	12.	INERTIA	L.	Tendency to remain at rest or resist motion or change
S	13.	INCIPIENT	M.	Act of atoning for sins or wrongdoing
M	14.	EXPIATION	N.	Burdensome; oppressive; troublesome; causing hardship
A	15.	DEFIANCE	O.	Person skilled in an applied art; craftsman
C	16.	SMARTING	P.	Capable of being easily communicated or transmitted
I	17.	TRIVIALITIES	Q.	Severe in manner or appearance; strict
T	18.	DISCLOSE	R.	Prostitute or paramour, esp. one associating with noblemen
D	19.	PREDECESSOR	S.	Beginning to exist or appear
P	20.	COMMUNICABLE	T.	Make known; reveal; uncover

UNIT RESOURCE MATERIALS

BULLETIN BOARD IDEAS *Siddhartha*

1. Save one corner of the board for the best of students' writing assignments.
2. Take one of the word search puzzles from the unit resources section of the LitPlan and copy it over in a large size onto the bulletin board. Write the words to find on one side. Invite students prior to and after class to find the words and circle them on the board.
3. Write several of the most significant quotations from the book onto the board on brightly colored paper. Invite students to write appropriate comments or their thoughts about the quotes under them on the board.
4. Outline the Hero's Journey for *Siddhartha* according to Joseph Campbell's model.
5. Make a bulletin board about the Four Noble Truths and the Eightfold Noble Path followed in Buddhism.
6. Make a bulletin board about the historical Siddhartha Gautama.
7. Invite students to submit their narrative poems to be posted on the bulletin board.
8. Create a bulletin board dedicated to the poems used in the unit: "A Dialogue of Self and Soul," "Song of Myself," and "Beau Fleuve."
9. Make characterization posters that highlight various traits of the characters in the novel, and fill them in as the class reads the story. Add traits discovered after each day's reading.
10. Make a board dedicated to Hermann Hesse's use of figurative language in the book (simile, metaphor, symbolism, personification, imagery, epithet). Have students add examples to the board as the find them in their reading.
11. Create a bulletin board dedicated to the symbolism of the river and/or the snake.

RELATED TOPICS *Siddhartha*

1. Siddhartha Gautama
2. Rivers as Symbols in Literature
3. Samanas
4. History of Dice Games
5. Parenting
6. Fathers and Sons
7. Eightfold Noble Path
8. Four Noble Truths
9. Brahmins
10. Caste System
11. Karma
12. Reincarnation
13. East Indian Culture
14. Buddhism
15. Snake Symbolism in Literature

MORE ACTIVITIES *Siddhartha*

1. Have students work together to make a timeline chronology of the events in the story. Take a large piece of construction or bulletin board paper and write the story events on it, either as students read or at the end of the unit as a summary. Students may add drawings or cut-out pictures to represent the events as well as a written statement.
2. Have students design a book cover (front, back, and inside flaps) for *Siddhartha*.
3. Have students choose one section of the book (with sufficient "dialogue") to rewrite as a play. In conjunction with this assignment, have students write a composition explaining the difficulties they encountered in changing from one written form to another.
4. Have students create a board game that outlines the journey of Siddhartha, being sure to incorporate terms from Joseph Campbell's Hero's Journey.
5. Discuss the principles of meditation with your students and take part of one class period to allow students to experience meditation. Perhaps have a guest speaker who is an authority on the subject come in and do meditative exercises with your students.
6. Tell your students to imagine they are casting a film version of *Siddhartha*. Have students make a list of actors and actresses who would best suit the available roles. Students should justify their choices.

UNIT WORD LIST *Siddhartha*

No.	Word	Clue/Definition
1.	BIRD	Siddhartha dreamed that it died and he threw it away.
2.	BOAT	Siddhartha's son's means of escape
3.	BRAHMIN	Siddhartha's father is one.
4.	BUDDHA	He is recognized by his complete peacefulness.
5.	CLEVERNESS	Buddha warns Siddhartha about too much of this.
6.	DEATH	Siddhartha longs for it after leaving Kamala.
7.	DICE	Siddhartha became obsessed with this game.
8.	EXPERIENCE	Siddhartha believes he must gain this for himself.
9.	FATHER	Siddhartha saw him in his river reflection.
10.	FINDING	It means being receptive without a goal.
11.	GOTAMA	The Buddha
12.	GOVINDA	Faithful friend of Siddhartha since childhood
13.	HERON	One of the two animals Siddhartha associated himself with
14.	HYPNOTIZES	Siddhartha does this to the eldest Samana.
15.	JETAVANA	The Buddha was given this place in which to live.
16.	KAMALA	Courtesan who loved Siddhartha
17.	KAMASWAMI	Businessman who befriended Siddhartha
18.	KNOWLEDGE	Siddhartha's journey was to acquire this.
19.	LOVE	The Buddha forbade his followers to bind themselves to this.
20.	OM	Word-sound that brings Siddhartha a sense of peace
21.	RIVER	It symbolizes the flow of life.
22.	SAMANAS	Siddhartha and Govinda joined them.
23.	SEEKING	It means having a goal.
24.	SELF	Siddhartha desires to lose this.
25.	SIDDHARTHA	Son of a Brahmin who left home to find enlightenment
26.	SNAKE	It symbolizes the transformation of Siddhartha.
27.	SON	He steals a boat and runs away.
28.	STONE	Siddhartha tells Govinda that it could one day become a man.
29.	TEACHERS	Siddhartha lost the desire to have these.
30.	TIME	The secret from the river: there is no such thing as ___
31.	TOWNSPEOPLE	They loved and admired Siddhartha.
32.	VASUDEVA	He taught Siddhartha about the river.
33.	WOODS	Where the Ferryman goes to die

WORD SEARCH - Siddhartha

```
S I D D H A R T H A J K F B U D D H A M
S D H G V C C M V X D L E R M K H E K Z
E A R Z Y S M C A Y E Y R A D K Y X N G
N Z M W O O D S S S J N R H D S P P O M
R S J A J J C R U Z J D Y M Y V N E W Q
E E T F N H Q K D T S F M I G C O R L T
V E X O R A X X E K E X A N M K T I E N
E K J Z N M S K V S C A N F M G I E D D
L I B B J E V J A F B T C T K F Z N G R
C N S J C M N L W Z Y P Q H C M E C E L
V G T O W N S P E O P L E A E Q S E Z Y
Z V P S N F R L V L L Y D F P R V V K C
K J D Q D F A S T R R N M H K G S S A D
L A E F M Y B T M W I G Q E D Q P F M D
W H M T C D O B H V V N B R G I Q Z A V
S W C A A V A H O E E I V O Z O C Y S S
K T H D L V T G H T R D H N T E T E W Z
F Z D X V A A I B D Z N F T V C T A A J
C D X G E P T N M V W I D O K K L N M N
C O M D S O N J A E N F L S N A K E I A
```

BIRD	FERRYMAN	KNOWLEDGE	SON
BOAT	FINDING	LOVE	STONE
BRAHMIN	GOTAMA	OM	TEACHERS
BUDDHA	GOVINDA	RIVER	TIME
CLEVERNESS	HERON	SAMANAS	TOWNSPEOPLE
DEATH	HYPNOTIZES	SEEKING	VASUDEVA
DICE	JETAVANA	SELF	WOODS
EXPERIENCE	KAMALA	SIDDHARTHA	
FATHER	KAMASWAMI	SNAKE	

WORD SEARCH ANSWER KEY - Siddhartha

BIRD	FERRYMAN	KNOWLEDGE	SON
BOAT	FINDING	LOVE	STONE
BRAHMIN	GOTAMA	OM	TEACHERS
BUDDHA	GOVINDA	RIVER	TIME
CLEVERNESS	HERON	SAMANAS	TOWNSPEOPLE
DEATH	HYPNOTIZES	SEEKING	VASUDEVA
DICE	JETAVANA	SELF	WOODS
EXPERIENCE	KAMALA	SIDDHARTHA	
FATHER	KAMASWAMI	SNAKE	

CROSSWORD - Siddhartha

Across
1. It symbolizes the transformation of Siddhartha.
3. Siddhartha dreamed that it died and he threw it away.
5. Siddhartha saw him in his river reflection.
6. Word-sound that brings Siddhartha a sense of peace
8. He taught Siddhartha about the river.
11. One of the two animals Siddhartha associates himself with
13. Courtesan who loved Siddhartha
14. He steals a boat and runs away.
16. Faithful friend of Siddhartha since childhood
17. Siddhartha's son's means of escape
20. Where the Ferryman goes to die.
21. Siddhartha became obsessed with this game.
22. Secret from the river: there is no such thing as ___.
23. The Buddha was given this place in which to live.

Down
1. Siddhartha desires to lose this.
2. Businessman who befriended Siddhartha
3. Siddhartha's father is one.
4. It symbolizes the flow of life.
5. It means being receptive without a goal.
7. Siddhartha and Govinda joined them.
9. Taught Siddhartha about the river
10. They loved and admired Siddhartha.
12. Buddha warns Siddhartha about too much of this.
15. Siddhartha's journey was to acquire this.
16. The Buddha
17. He is recognized by his complete peacefulness.
18. Siddhartha longs for it after leaving Kamala.
19. The Buddha forbade his followers to bind themselves to this.

CROSSWORD ANSWER KEY - Siddhartha

Across
1. It symbolizes the transformation of Siddhartha.
3. Siddhartha dreamed that it died and he threw it away.
5. Siddhartha saw him in his river reflection.
6. Word-sound that brings Siddhartha a sense of peace
8. He taught Siddhartha about the river.
11. One of the two animals Siddhartha associates himself with
13. Courtesan who loved Siddhartha
14. He steals a boat and runs away.
16. Faithful friend of Siddhartha since childhood
17. Siddhartha's son's means of escape
20. Where the Ferryman goes to die.
21. Siddhartha became obsessed with this game.
22. Secret from the river: there is no such thing as ___.
23. The Buddha was given this place in which to live.

Down
1. Siddhartha desires to lose this.
2. Businessman who befriended Siddhartha
3. Siddhartha's father is one.
4. It symbolizes the flow of life.
5. It means being receptive without a goal.
7. Siddhartha and Govinda joined them.
9. Taught Siddhartha about the river
10. They loved and admired Siddhartha.
12. Buddha warns Siddhartha about too much of this.
15. Siddhartha's journey was to acquire this.
16. The Buddha
17. He is recognized by his complete peacefulness.
18. Siddhartha longs for it after leaving Kamala.
19. The Buddha forbade his followers to bind themselves to this.

MATCHING 1 *Siddhartha*

____ 1. SEEKING   A. Siddhartha lost the desire to have these.
____ 2. WOODS   B. The secret from the river: there is no such thing as ___
____ 3. RIVER   C. The Buddha
____ 4. SAMANAS   D. Businessman who befriended Siddhartha
____ 5. VASUDEVA   E. Son of a Brahmin who left home to find enlightenment
____ 6. KAMASWAMI   F. The Buddha forbade his followers to bind themselves to this.
____ 7. KAMALA   G. One of the two animals Siddhartha associated himself with
____ 8. GOTAMA   H. It symbolizes the flow of life.
____ 9. GOVINDA   I. He taught Siddhartha about the river.
____ 10. STONE   J. Faithful friend of Siddhartha since childhood
____ 11. LOVE   K. Siddhartha tells Govinda that it could one day become a man.
____ 12. FINDING   L. It means having a goal.
____ 13. TIME   M. It symbolizes the transformation of Siddhartha.
____ 14. BIRD   N. Siddhartha and Govinda joined them.
____ 15. TEACHERS   O. It means being receptive without a goal.
____ 16. BUDDHA   P. He is recognized by his complete peacefulness.
____ 17. HERON   Q. Where the Ferryman goes to die
____ 18. BRAHMIN   R. Siddhartha dreamed that it died and he threw it away.
____ 19. SNAKE   S. Courtesan who loved Siddhartha
____ 20. SIDDHARTHA   T. Siddhartha's father is one.

MATCHING 1 ANSWER KEY *Siddhartha*

L	1.	SEEKING	A.	Siddhartha lost the desire to have these.
Q	2.	WOODS	B.	The secret from the river: there is no such thing as ___
H	3.	RIVER	C.	The Buddha
N	4.	SAMANAS	D.	Businessman who befriended Siddhartha
I	5.	VASUDEVA	E.	Son of a Brahmin who left home to find enlightenment
D	6.	KAMASWAMI	F.	The Buddha forbade his followers to bind themselves to this.
S	7.	KAMALA	G.	One of the two animals Siddhartha associated himself with
C	8.	GOTAMA	H.	It symbolizes the flow of life.
J	9.	GOVINDA	I.	He taught Siddhartha about the river.
K	10.	STONE	J.	Faithful friend of Siddhartha since childhood
F	11.	LOVE	K.	Siddhartha tells Govinda that it could one day become a man.
O	12.	FINDING	L.	It means having a goal.
B	13.	TIME	M.	It symbolizes the transformation of Siddhartha.
R	14.	BIRD	N.	Siddhartha and Govinda joined them.
A	15.	TEACHERS	O.	It means being receptive without a goal.
P	16.	BUDDHA	P.	He is recognized by his complete peacefulness.
G	17.	HERON	Q.	Where the Ferryman goes to die
T	18.	BRAHMIN	R.	Siddhartha dreamed that it died and he threw it away.
M	19.	SNAKE	S.	Courtesan who loved Siddhartha
E	20.	SIDDHARTHA	T.	Siddhartha's father is one.

MATCHING 2 *Siddhartha*

____ 1. SIDDHARTHA   A. It symbolizes the transformation of Siddhartha.

____ 2. DEATH   B. Faithful friend of Siddhartha since childhood

____ 3. EXPERIENCE   C. He taught Siddhartha about the river.

____ 4. JETAVANA   D. Siddhartha desires to lose this.

____ 5. SON   E. Siddhartha and Govinda joined them.

____ 6. SELF   F. Courtesan who loved Siddhartha

____ 7. SNAKE   G. He is recognized by his complete peacefulness.

____ 8. BRAHMIN   H. Son of a Brahmin who left home to find enlightenment

____ 9. HERON   I. The Buddha was given this place in which to live.

____ 10. DICE   J. It symbolizes the flow of life.

____ 11. LOVE   K. Siddhartha longs for it after leaving Kamala.

____ 12. GOVINDA   L. He steals a boat and runs away.

____ 13. GOTAMA   M. Word-sound that brings Siddhartha a sense of peace

____ 14. KAMALA   N. Businessman who befriended Siddhartha

____ 15. KAMASWAMI   O. The Buddha forbade his followers to bind themselves to this.

____ 16. VASUDEVA   P. Siddhartha became obsessed with this game.

____ 17. SAMANAS   Q. The Buddha

____ 18. RIVER   R. Siddhartha believes he must gain this for himself.

____ 19. OM   S. Siddhartha's father is one.

____ 20. BUDDHA   T. One of the two animals Siddhartha associated himself with

MATCHING 2 ANSWER KEY *Siddhartha*

H	1.	SIDDHARTHA	A.	It symbolizes the transformation of Siddhartha.
K	2.	DEATH	B.	Faithful friend of Siddhartha since childhood
R	3.	EXPERIENCE	C.	He taught Siddhartha about the river.
I	4.	JETAVANA	D.	Siddhartha desires to lose this.
L	5.	SON	E.	Siddhartha and Govinda joined them.
D	6.	SELF	F.	Courtesan who loved Siddhartha
A	7.	SNAKE	G.	He is recognized by his complete peacefulness.
S	8.	BRAHMIN	H.	Son of a Brahmin who left home to find enlightenment
T	9.	HERON	I.	The Buddha was given this place in which to live.
P	10.	DICE	J.	It symbolizes the flow of life.
O	11.	LOVE	K.	Siddhartha longs for it after leaving Kamala.
B	12.	GOVINDA	L.	He steals a boat and runs away.
Q	13.	GOTAMA	M.	Word-sound that brings Siddhartha a sense of peace
F	14.	KAMALA	N.	Businessman who befriended Siddhartha
N	15.	KAMASWAMI	O.	The Buddha forbade his followers to bind themselves to this.
C	16.	VASUDEVA	P.	Siddhartha became obsessed with this game.
E	17.	SAMANAS	Q.	The Buddha
J	18.	RIVER	R.	Siddhartha believes he must gain this for himself.
M	19.	OM	S.	Siddhartha's father is one.
G	20.	BUDDHA	T.	One of the two animals Siddhartha associated himself with

JUGGLE LETTERS 1 *Siddhartha*

_____ = 1. IHRHTDADSA
   Son of a Brahmin who left home to find enlightenment

_____ = 2. EADTH
   Siddhartha longs for it after leaving Kamala.

_____ = 3. NCEXRIEEPE
   Siddhartha believes he must gain this for himself.

_____ = 4. TVAJENAA
   The Buddha was given this place in which to live.

_____ = 5. SLEF
   Siddhartha desires to lose this.

_____ = 6. EKNAS
   It symbolizes the transformation of Siddhartha.

_____ = 7. BINAMHR
   Siddhartha's father is one.

_____ = 8. REHNO
   One of the two animals Siddhartha associated himself with

_____ = 9. HUDDBA
   He is recognized by his complete peacefulness.

_____ = 10. ELVO
   The Buddha forbade his followers to bind themselves to this.

_____ = 11. NETOS
   Siddhartha tells Govinda that it could one day become a man.

_____ = 12. AIVNGOD
   Faithful friend of Siddhartha since childhood

_____ = 13. OMGATA
   The Buddha

_____ = 14. AKAMAL
   Courtesan who loved Siddhartha

_____ = 15. MIKASAMAW
   Businessman who befriended Siddhartha

_____ = 16. VSAAUEVD
   He taught Siddhartha about the river.

_____ = 17. AAMSSNA
   Siddhartha and Govinda joined them.

_____ = 18. VIRRE
   It symbolizes the flow of life.

_____ = 19. DWSOO
   Where the Ferryman goes to die

_____ = 20. TEMI
   The secret from the river: there is no such thing as ___

JUGGLE LETTERS 1 ANSWER KEY *Siddhartha*

SIDDHARTHA = 1. IHRHTDADSA
Son of a Brahmin who left home to find enlightenment

DEATH = 2. EADTH
Siddhartha longs for it after leaving Kamala.

EXPERIENCE = 3. NCEXRIEEPE
Siddhartha believes he must gain this for himself.

JETAVANA = 4. TVAJENAA
The Buddha was given this place in which to live.

SELF = 5. SLEF
Siddhartha desires to lose this.

SNAKE = 6. EKNAS
It symbolizes the transformation of Siddhartha.

BRAHMIN = 7. BINAMHR
Siddhartha's father is one.

HERON = 8. REHNO
One of the two animals Siddhartha associated himself with

BUDDHA = 9. HUDDBA
He is recognized by his complete peacefulness.

LOVE = 10. ELVO
The Buddha forbade his followers to bind themselves to this.

STONE = 11. NETOS
Siddhartha tells Govinda that it could one day become a man.

GOVINDA = 12. AIVNGOD
Faithful friend of Siddhartha since childhood

GOTAMA = 13. OMGATA
The Buddha

KAMALA = 14. AKAMAL
Courtesan who loved Siddhartha

KAMASWAMI = 15. MIKASAMAW
Businessman who befriended Siddhartha

VASUDEVA = 16. VSAAUEVD
He taught Siddhartha about the river.

SAMANAS = 17. AAMSSNA
Siddhartha and Govinda joined them.

RIVER = 18. VIRRE
It symbolizes the flow of life.

WOODS = 19. DWSOO
Where the Ferryman goes to die

TIME = 20. TEMI
The secret from the river: there is no such thing as ___

JUGGLE LETTERS 2 *Siddhartha*

_____ = 1. DTAHADRHIS
Son of a Brahmin who left home to find enlightenment

_____ = 2. BINHRMA
Siddhartha's father is one.

_____ = 3. NHEOR
One of the two animals Siddhartha associated himself with

_____ = 4. DDAHUB
He is recognized by his complete peacefulness.

_____ = 5. CEATSHER
Siddhartha lost the desire to have these.

_____ = 6. DIRB
Siddhartha dreamed that it died and he threw it away.

_____ = 7. IMET
The secret from the river: there is no such thing as ___

_____ = 8. NIGFDNI
It means being receptive without a goal.

_____ = 9. KSEEIGN
It means having a goal.

_____ = 10. SNKEA
It symbolizes the transformation of Siddhartha.

_____ = 11. LESF
Siddhartha desires to lose this.

_____ = 12. AGOVIDN
Faithful friend of Siddhartha since childhood

_____ = 13. GMTAOA
The Buddha

_____ = 14. AALAMK
Courtesan who loved Siddhartha

_____ = 15. AWSMAKIAM
Businessman who befriended Siddhartha

_____ = 16. VUSAVEDA
He taught Siddhartha about the river.

_____ = 17. AASAMNS
Siddhartha and Govinda joined them.

_____ = 18. RIRVE
It symbolizes the flow of life.

_____ = 19. JNAVTEAA
The Buddha was given this place in which to live.

_____ = 20. ATBO
Siddhartha's son's means of escape

JUGGLE LETTERS 2 ANSWER KEY *Siddhartha*

SIDDHARTHA	= 1.	DTAHADRHIS Son of a Brahmin who left home to find enlightenment
BRAHMIN	= 2.	BINHRMA Siddhartha's father is one.
HERON	= 3.	NHEOR One of the two animals Siddhartha associated himself with
BUDDHA	= 4.	DDAHUB He is recognized by his complete peacefulness.
TEACHERS	= 5.	CEATSHER Siddhartha lost the desire to have these.
BIRD	= 6.	DIRB Siddhartha dreamed that it died and he threw it away.
TIME	= 7.	IMET The secret from the river: there is no such thing as ___
FINDING	= 8.	NIGFDNI It means being receptive without a goal.
SEEKING	= 9.	KSEEIGN It means having a goal.
SNAKE	= 10.	SNKEA It symbolizes the transformation of Siddhartha.
SELF	= 11.	LESF Siddhartha desires to lose this.
GOVINDA	= 12.	AGOVIDN Faithful friend of Siddhartha since childhood
GOTAMA	= 13.	GMTAOA The Buddha
KAMALA	= 14.	AALAMK Courtesan who loved Siddhartha
KAMASWAMI	= 15.	AWSMAKIAM Businessman who befriended Siddhartha
VASUDEVA	= 16.	VUSAVEDA He taught Siddhartha about the river.
SAMANAS	= 17.	AASAMNS Siddhartha and Govinda joined them.
RIVER	= 18.	RIRVE It symbolizes the flow of life.
JETAVANA	= 19.	JNAVTEAA The Buddha was given this place in which to live.
BOAT	= 20.	ATBO Siddhartha's son's means of escape

VOCABULARY RESOURCE MATERIALS

Siddhartha Vocabulary

No.	Word	Clue/Definition
1.	ALMS	Money, food, or other donations given to the poor
2.	ARDENT	Characterized by intense feeling
3.	ARTISAN	Person skilled in an applied art; craftsman
4.	ASCETICS	Those who renounce material comforts & lead a life of self-discipline
5.	ASSIDUOUS	Constant in effort; working diligently at a task
6.	AUSTERE	Severe in manner or appearance; strict
7.	AVARICIOUS	Immoderately desirous of wealth or gain; greedy
8.	CHASM	Deep cleft in the ground; gorge
9.	COMMUNICABLE	Capable of being easily communicated or transmitted
10.	COMPELLED	Forced to submit; subdued
11.	CONSIDERATION	Thoughtful or sympathetic regard or respect
12.	COURTESAN	Prostitute or paramour, esp. one associating with noblemen
13.	DAINTY	Pleasing to the taste, and often temptingly served or delicate
14.	DECLIVITY	Downward slope
15.	DEFIANCE	Bold resistance to authority or any opposing force
16.	DEMEANOR	Conduct; behavior; attitude
17.	DEVOUT	Pious; religious; devoted to divine worship or service
18.	DISCLOSE	Make known; reveal; uncover
19.	DISILLUSIONMENT	A state of being freed from false beliefs
20.	DISPEL	Cause to vanish; get rid of
21.	DIVERSITIES	Points or aspects in which things differ
22.	EMANATED	Flowed out from; came from
23.	ENNUI	Boredom; dissatisfaction resulting from lack of interest
24.	EQUANIMITY	Quality of being calm and even-tempered; composure
25.	ERUDITION	Knowledge acquired by study; learning
26.	ESTEEMED	Respected
27.	EXPIATION	Act of atoning for sins or wrongdoing
28.	FESTER	Infect, inflame, or corrupt
29.	GUILD	Association of tradesmen
30.	HASTINESS	With overly-eager speed and possible carelessness
31.	HINDRANCE	Obstruction; something in the way or a burden
32.	IMPERTURBABLE	Can't be bothered, agitated, or upset
33.	INCIPIENT	Beginning to exist or appear
34.	INDIGNATION	Anger aroused by something unjust, mean, or unworthy
35.	INDOLENT	Inactive; lethargic
36.	INERTIA	Tendency to remain at rest or resist motion or change
37.	INSATIABLE	Incapable of being satisfied or appeased
38.	INTRINSIC	Belonging to a thing by its very nature

No.	Word	Clue/Definition
39.	IRREFUTABLY	Undeniably; unarguably
40.	LAMENT	Feel or express sorrow or regret
41.	MUTILATE	Injure or disfigure by removing or irreparably damaging parts
42.	ONEROUS	Burdensome; oppressive; troublesome; causing hardship
43.	OSTRACIZED	Excluded from a group
44.	PALLIATIVE	Something that makes pain or sorrow easier to bear
45.	PREDECESSOR	One who came before another in holding an office or position
46.	PRUDENT	Wise or judicious in practical affairs
47.	RENOUNCED	Gave up or put aside voluntarily
48.	SANCTUARY	Sacred or holy place; place of safety
49.	SENILE	Of or belonging to old age or aged persons
50.	SERVILE	Characteristic of, proper to, or customary for slaves
51.	SMARTING	Hurting with a sharp, usually superficial, stinging pain
52.	SOJOURN	Temporary stay; brief period of residence
53.	STRIVE	Try hard
54.	SUBMERGED	Sunk below the surface
55.	TENACIOUS	Persistent; stubborn
56.	TRANSITORY	Not lasting, permanent, or eternal
57.	TRIVIALITIES	Things that are unimportant or frivolous
58.	VENERABLENESS	Quality of commanding respect by virtue of age, character, or position
59.	WRETCHED	Miserable; very unfortunate

VOCABULARY WORD SEARCH - Siddhartha

```
A S A N C T U A R Y I D E C N U O N E R
R S B S L O H Q S F N I I S Q J P D V T
T E S S C P U P Z E T S H S T K B C I S
I N I I T E F R Y S R P I A C E F K R C
S E N M D R T S T T I E N U L L E W T M
A L D U S U I I B E N L D S J A O M S T
N B O T M D O V C R S P R T H T M S E R
R A L I A I S U I S I A A E N E I E E D
U R E L R T E Z S A C F N R R N S D N K
O E N A T I I N Y K L D C E E A U A L T
J N T T I O T N D A F I E R S C O I Y M
O E D E N N I B V E N N T N Y I R N F F
S V Q K G L S A K N M I T I E O E T D C
D E H C T E R W K B A E G M E U N Y Y E
N F Z M P I E D E Z I C A R T S O S L T
R Q H C C N V Q I U N N E N M Q Q I N M
E X P I A T I O N Z A D R L O W V E S Y
P X O P R U D E N T B S A S L R D A J Z
G U I L D E L L E P M O C K E R H W V M
S E N I L E Q D E V O U T S A C Y W K F
```

ALMS	DIVERSITIES	OSTRACIZED
ARDENT	EMANATED	PRUDENT
ARTISAN	ENNUI	RENOUNCED
ASCETICS	ERUDITION	SANCTUARY
ASSIDUOUS	ESTEEMED	SENILE
AUSTERE	EXPIATION	SERVILE
AVARICIOUS	FESTER	SMARTING
CHASM	GUILD	SOJOURN
COMPELLED	HINDRANCE	STRIVE
COURTESAN	INDOLENT	TENACIOUS
DAINTY	INERTIA	TRIVIALITIES
DEMEANOR	INTRINSIC	VENERABLENESS
DEVOUT	LAMENT	WRETCHED
DISCLOSE	MUTILATE	
DISPEL	ONEROUS	

VOCABULARY WORD SEARCH ANSWER KEY - Siddhartha

ALMS	DIVERSITIES	OSTRACIZED
ARDENT	EMANATED	PRUDENT
ARTISAN	ENNUI	RENOUNCED
ASCETICS	ERUDITION	SANCTUARY
ASSIDUOUS	ESTEEMED	SENILE
AUSTERE	EXPIATION	SERVILE
AVARICIOUS	FESTER	SMARTING
CHASM	GUILD	SOJOURN
COMPELLED	HINDRANCE	STRIVE
COURTESAN	INDOLENT	TENACIOUS
DAINTY	INERTIA	TRIVIALITIES
DEMEANOR	INTRINSIC	VENERABLENESS
DEVOUT	LAMENT	WRETCHED
DISCLOSE	MUTILATE	
DISPEL	ONEROUS	

VOCABULARY CROSSWORD PUZZLE - Siddhartha

Across
1. Boredom; dissatisfaction resulting from lack of interest
3. Constant in effort; working diligently on a task
5. Association of tradesmen
7. Flowed out from; came from
10. Characteristic of, proper to, or customary for slaves
13. Gave up or put aside voluntarily
15. Pleasing to the taste and often temptingly served or delicate
16. Money, food, or other donations given to the poor
18. Incapable of being satisfied or appeased
21. Obstruction; something in the way or a burden
23. Tendency to remain at rest or resist motion or change
24. Bold resistance to authority or any opposing force
25. Forced or driven to a course of action

Down
1. Respected
2. Inactive; lethargic
4. Of or belonging to old age or aged persons
6. Pious; religious; devoted to divine worship or service
8. Knowledge acquired by study; learning
9. Immoderately desirous of wealth; greedy
11. Miserable; very unfortunate
12. Anger aroused by something unjust, mean, or unworthy
14. Cause to vanish; get rid of
17. Wise or judicious in practical affairs
19. Hurting with a sharp, usually superficial, stinging pain
20. Feel or express sorrow or regret
22. Try hard

VOCABULARY CROSSWORD PUZZLE ANSWER KEY - Siddhartha

Across
1. Boredom; dissatisfaction resulting from lack of interest
3. Constant in effort; working diligently on a task
5. Association of tradesmen
7. Flowed out from; came from
10. Characteristic of, proper to, or customary for slaves
13. Gave up or put aside voluntarily
15. Pleasing to the taste and often temptingly served or delicate
16. Money, food, or other donations given to the poor
18. Incapable of being satisfied or appeased
21. Obstruction; something in the way or a burden
23. Tendency to remain at rest or resist motion or change
24. Bold resistance to authority or any opposing force
25. Forced or driven to a course of action

Down
1. Respected
2. Inactive; lethargic
4. Of or belonging to old age or aged persons
6. Pious; religious; devoted to divine worship or service
8. Knowledge acquired by study; learning
9. Immoderately desirous of wealth; greedy
11. Miserable; very unfortunate
12. Anger aroused by something unjust, mean, or unworthy
14. Cause to vanish; get rid of
17. Wise or judicious in practical affairs
19. Hurting with a sharp, usually superficial, stinging pain
20. Feel or express sorrow or regret
22. Try hard

VOCABULARY MATCHING 1 *Siddhartha*

____ 1. ALMS   A. Incapable of being satisfied or appeased

____ 2. OSTRACIZED   B. Hurting with a sharp, usually superficial, stinging pain

____ 3. PREDECESSOR   C. Undeniably; unarguably

____ 4. RENOUNCED   D. Thoughtful or sympathetic regard or respect

____ 5. SENILE   E. Try hard

____ 6. SMARTING   F. Gave up or put aside voluntarily

____ 7. STRIVE   G. Person skilled in an applied art; craftsman

____ 8. TENACIOUS   H. Capable of being easily communicated or transmitted

____ 9. TRIVIALITIES   I. Persistent; stubborn

____ 10. MUTILATE   J. Pleasing to the taste, and often temptingly served or delicate

____ 11. IRREFUTABLY   K. Injure or disfigure by removing or irreparably damaging parts

____ 12. ARTISAN   L. Things that are unimportant or frivolous

____ 13. ASSIDUOUS   M. One who came before another in holding an office or position

____ 14. AVARICIOUS   N. Constant in effort; working diligently at a task

____ 15. COMMUNICABLE   O. Of or belonging to old age or aged persons

____ 16. CONSIDERATION   P. Excluded from a group

____ 17. DAINTY   Q. Money, food, or other donations given to the poor

____ 18. DEFIANCE   R. Immoderately desirous of wealth or gain; greedy

____ 19. INSATIABLE   S. Bold resistance to authority or any opposing force

____ 20. WRETCHED   T. Miserable; very unfortunate

VOCABULARY MATCHING 1 ANSWER KEY *Siddhartha*

Q	1.	ALMS	A.	Incapable of being satisfied or appeased
P	2.	OSTRACIZED	B.	Hurting with a sharp, usually superficial, stinging pain
M	3.	PREDECESSOR	C.	Undeniably; unarguably
F	4.	RENOUNCED	D.	Thoughtful or sympathetic regard or respect
O	5.	SENILE	E.	Try hard
B	6.	SMARTING	F.	Gave up or put aside voluntarily
E	7.	STRIVE	G.	Person skilled in an applied art; craftsman
I	8.	TENACIOUS	H.	Capable of being easily communicated or transmitted
L	9.	TRIVIALITIES	I.	Persistent; stubborn
K	10.	MUTILATE	J.	Pleasing to the taste, and often temptingly served or delicate
C	11.	IRREFUTABLY	K.	Injure or disfigure by removing or irreparably damaging parts
G	12.	ARTISAN	L.	Things that are unimportant or frivolous
N	13.	ASSIDUOUS	M.	One who came before another in holding an office or position
R	14.	AVARICIOUS	N.	Constant in effort; working diligently at a task
H	15.	COMMUNICABLE	O.	Of or belonging to old age or aged persons
D	16.	CONSIDERATION	P.	Excluded from a group
J	17.	DAINTY	Q.	Money, food, or other donations given to the poor
S	18.	DEFIANCE	R.	Immoderately desirous of wealth or gain; greedy
A	19.	INSATIABLE	S.	Bold resistance to authority or any opposing force
T	20.	WRETCHED	T.	Miserable; very unfortunate

VOCABULARY MATCHING 2 *Siddhartha*

___ 1. PRUDENT   A. Respected
___ 2. COMPELLED   B. Anger aroused by something unjust, mean, or unworthy
___ 3. CHASM   C. Feel or express sorrow or regret
___ 4. AUSTERE   D. Severe in manner or appearance; strict
___ 5. ASCETICS   E. Not lasting, permanent, or eternal
___ 6. ARDENT   F. Something that makes pain or sorrow easier to bear
___ 7. SANCTUARY   G. Downward slope
___ 8. SOJOURN   H. Forced or driven to a course of action
___ 9. TRANSITORY   I. Quality of commanding respect by virtue of age, character, or position
___ 10. COURTESAN   J. Characterized by intense feeling
___ 11. DECLIVITY   K. Cause to vanish; get rid of
___ 12. PALLIATIVE   L. With overly-eager speed and possible carelessness
___ 13. LAMENT   M. Temporary stay; brief period of residence
___ 14. INERTIA   N. Those who renounce material comforts & lead a life of self-discipline
___ 15. INDIGNATION   O. Tendency to remain at rest or resist motion or change
___ 16. IMPERTURBABLE   P. Can't be bothered, agitated, or upset
___ 17. HASTINESS   Q. Wise or judicious in practical affairs
___ 18. ESTEEMED   R. Deep cleft in the ground; gorge
___ 19. DISPEL   S. Prostitute or paramour, esp. one associating with noblemen
___ 20. VENERABLENESS   T. Sacred or holy place; place of safety

VOCABULARY MATCHING 2 ANSWER KEY *Siddhartha*

Q	1.	PRUDENT	A.	Respected
H	2.	COMPELLED	B.	Anger aroused by something unjust, mean, or unworthy
R	3.	CHASM	C.	Feel or express sorrow or regret
D	4.	AUSTERE	D.	Severe in manner or appearance; strict
N	5.	ASCETICS	E.	Not lasting, permanent, or eternal
J	6.	ARDENT	F.	Something that makes pain or sorrow easier to bear
T	7.	SANCTUARY	G.	Downward slope
M	8.	SOJOURN	H.	Forced or driven to a course of action
E	9.	TRANSITORY	I.	Quality of commanding respect by virtue of age, character, or position
S	10.	COURTESAN	J.	Characterized by intense feeling
G	11.	DECLIVITY	K.	Cause to vanish; get rid of
F	12.	PALLIATIVE	L.	With overly-eager speed and possible carelessness
C	13.	LAMENT	M.	Temporary stay; brief period of residence
O	14.	INERTIA	N.	Those who renounce material comforts & lead a life of self-discipline
B	15.	INDIGNATION	O.	Tendency to remain at rest or resist motion or change
P	16.	IMPERTURBABLE	P.	Can't be bothered, agitated, or upset
L	17.	HASTINESS	Q.	Wise or judicious in practical affairs
A	18.	ESTEEMED	R.	Deep cleft in the ground; gorge
K	19.	DISPEL	S.	Prostitute or paramour, esp. one associating with noblemen
I	20.	VENERABLENESS	T.	Sacred or holy place; place of safety

VOCABULARY JUGGLE LETTERS 1 *Siddhartha*

_____ = 1. ICOARVIASU
Immoderately desirous of wealth or gain; greedy

_____ = 2. NADRENHCI
Obstruction; something in the way or a burden

_____ = 3. NIEINTCPI
Beginning to exist or appear

_____ = 4. NNOLDITE
Inactive; lethargic

_____ = 5. TNEISAILBA
Incapable of being satisfied or appeased

_____ = 6. ATELTIUM
Injure or disfigure by removing or irreparably damaging parts

_____ = 7. DPSREOECRSE
One who came before another in holding an office or position

_____ = 8. RGTMANSI
Hurting with a sharp, usually superficial, stinging pain

_____ = 9. BDSEGMREU
Sunk below the surface

_____ = 10. IUDLG
Association of tradesmen

_____ = 11. POTIIAXNE
Act of atoning for sins or wrongdoing

_____ = 12. OSINAONIERTCD
Thoughtful or sympathetic regard or respect

_____ = 13. URNATESCO
Prostitute or paramour, esp. one associating with noblemen

_____ = 14. VCYLTEIID
Downward slope

_____ = 15. OTDEVU
Pious; religious; devoted to divine worship or service

_____ = 16. OMNULSLEIIIDTNS
A state of being freed from false beliefs

_____ = 17. SDIEVRSEIIT
Points or aspects in which things differ

_____ = 18. NUENI
Boredom; dissatisfaction resulting from lack of interest

_____ = 19. UODITEIRN
Knowledge acquired by study; learning

_____ = 20. ROTNIYTRAS
Not lasting, permanent, or eternal

VOCABULARY JUGGLE LETTERS 1 ANSWER KEY *Siddhartha*

AVARICIOUS	= 1.	ICOARVIASU Immoderately desirous of wealth or gain; greedy
HINDRANCE	= 2.	NADRENHCI Obstruction; something in the way or a burden
INCIPIENT	= 3.	NIEINTCPI Beginning to exist or appear
INDOLENT	= 4.	NNOLDITE Inactive; lethargic
INSATIABLE	= 5.	TNEISAILBA Incapable of being satisfied or appeased
MUTILATE	= 6.	ATELTIUM Injure or disfigure by removing or irreparably damaging parts
PREDECESSOR	= 7.	DPSREOECRSE One who came before another in holding an office or position
SMARTING	= 8.	RGTMANSI Hurting with a sharp, usually superficial, stinging pain
SUBMERGED	= 9.	BDSEGMREU Sunk below the surface
GUILD	= 10.	IUDLG Association of tradesmen
EXPIATION	= 11.	POTIIAXNE Act of atoning for sins or wrongdoing
CONSIDERATION	= 12.	OSINAONIERTCD Thoughtful or sympathetic regard or respect
COURTESAN	= 13.	URNATESCO Prostitute or paramour, esp. one associating with noblemen
DECLIVITY	= 14.	VCYLTEIID Downward slope
DEVOUT	= 15.	OTDEVU Pious; religious; devoted to divine worship or service
DISILLUSIONMENT	= 16.	OMNULSLEIIIDTNS A state of being freed from false beliefs
DIVERSITIES	= 17.	SDIEVRSEIIT Points or aspects in which things differ
ENNUI	= 18.	NUENI Boredom; dissatisfaction resulting from lack of interest
ERUDITION	= 19.	UODITEIRN Knowledge acquired by study; learning
TRANSITORY	= 20.	ROTNIYTRAS Not lasting, permanent, or eternal

VOCABULARY JUGGLE LETTERS 2 *Siddhartha*

_____ = 1. ISECSACT
Those who renounce material comforts & lead a life of self-discipline

_____ = 2. NTCPENIII
Beginning to exist or appear

_____ = 3. LIEOTNND
Inactive; lethargic

_____ = 4. ASZOCDTEIR
Excluded from a group

_____ = 5. VELILAPTAI
Something that makes pain or sorrow easier to bear

_____ = 6. TPEDRUN
Wise or judicious in practical affairs

_____ = 7. DENCRUOEN
Gave up or put aside voluntarily

_____ = 8. RVELESI
Characteristic of, proper to, or customary for slaves

_____ = 9. TCNIESOAU
Persistent; stubborn

_____ = 10. BRLUEPEMBTIRA
Can't be bothered, agitated, or upset

_____ = 11. DHNEIRCNA
Obstruction; something in the way or a burden

_____ = 12. RAEUSTE
Severe in manner or appearance; strict

_____ = 13. ORIUIACAVS
Immoderately desirous of wealth or gain; greedy

_____ = 14. LUBOAMIECCMN
Capable of being easily communicated or transmitted

_____ = 15. TENRONIDIOCAS
Thoughtful or sympathetic regard or respect

_____ = 16. FEACIEDN
Bold resistance to authority or any opposing force

_____ = 17. ILNMSTIELLSUIDNO
A state of being freed from false beliefs

_____ = 18. YMTAUIIENQ
Quality of being calm and even-tempered; composure

_____ = 19. IRIONTDUE
Knowledge acquired by study; learning

_____ = 20. ITSRYNOTRA
Not lasting, permanent, or eternal

VOCABULARY JUGGLE LETTERS 2 ANSWER KEY *Siddhartha*

ASCETICS	= 1.	ISECSACT Those who renounce material comforts & lead a life of self-discipline
INCIPIENT	= 2.	NTCPENIII Beginning to exist or appear
INDOLENT	= 3.	LIEOTNND Inactive; lethargic
OSTRACIZED	= 4.	ASZOCDTEIR Excluded from a group
PALLIATIVE	= 5.	VELILAPTAI Something that makes pain or sorrow easier to bear
PRUDENT	= 6.	TPEDRUN Wise or judicious in practical affairs
RENOUNCED	= 7.	DENCRUOEN Gave up or put aside voluntarily
SERVILE	= 8.	RVELESI Characteristic of, proper to, or customary for slaves
TENACIOUS	= 9.	TCNIESOAU Persistent; stubborn
IMPERTURBABLE	= 10.	BRLUEPEMBTIRA Can't be bothered, agitated, or upset
HINDRANCE	= 11.	DHNEIRCNA Obstruction; something in the way or a burden
AUSTERE	= 12.	RAEUSTE Severe in manner or appearance; strict
AVARICIOUS	= 13.	ORIUIACAVS Immoderately desirous of wealth or gain; greedy
COMMUNICABLE	= 14.	LUBOAMIECCMN Capable of being easily communicated or transmitted
CONSIDERATION	= 15.	TENRONIDIOCAS Thoughtful or sympathetic regard or respect
DEFIANCE	= 16.	FEACIEDN Bold resistance to authority or any opposing force
DISILLUSIONMENT	= 17.	ILNMSTIELSUIDNO A state of being freed from false beliefs
EQUANIMITY	= 18.	YMTAUIIENQ Quality of being calm and even-tempered; composure
ERUDITION	= 19.	IRIONTDUE Knowledge acquired by study; learning
TRANSITORY	= 20.	ITSRYNOTRA Not lasting, permanent, or eternal

www.ingramcontent.com/pod-product-compliance
Lightning Source LLC
Chambersburg PA
CBHW051405070526
44584CB00023B/3303